OFFICERS and SOLDIERS

THE FRENCH IMPERIAL GUARD 1804-1815

Volume 4
The Cavalry

Part Three

André JOUINEAU

translated from the French by
Alan McKAY

HISTOIRE & COLLECTIONS

The CAVALRY of the IMPERIAL GUARD

We begin this fourth volume with the end of the chapter devoted to the *Gendarmes d'Elite*. We will then consider those cavalry units of the Guard which are much less known: the Gendarmes d'Ordonnance (the Ordnance Gendarmes), the Gardes d'Honneur (the Guards of Honour), the Lithuanian Tartars, the Krakus and the Eclaireurs (Scouts). Finally in the last chapter, we will start our study of the Horse Artillery which will be developed further in Volume V.

The Gendarmes d'ordonnance

On 24 September 1806, the Emperor sent a letter to the Minister of the Interior: *"Monsieur Champagny, you will find attached an idea for a circular which you can set out as you wish. You will communicate it to Minister Dejean so that he can send it to Maréchal Kellermann."* The project he had in mind was to recruit and set up a new corps, the Gendarmes d'Ordonnance. Napoleon continued: *"I do not know what will come of it. You know that I do not need troops, but I do wish to open up this career again to all those who have been cut off from the motherland by the circumstances of the Revolution; after all, it is such a natural career for any Frenchman. If you adopt these measures, you will have to write immediately to the Prefects of Paris and the neighbouring departments."*

It is easy to see that the idea behind this was political: an attempt by Napoleon to attract the sons of émigré families which had returned to France. He entertained the hope that he would be able to make them into an elite unit for his household, even to re-establish the Compagnies de Gardes du Corps (Life Guard Companies) as they were under the Ancien Régime. The reasons for him doing this were confirmed in a letter addressed to Maréchal Kellermann on 25 October 1806: *"(...) By organising this corps, I have been influenced more by political than by military considerations (...)."*

He also stipulated what the entry conditions were and how the corps was to be organised: *"(...) Any man between 18 and 40, who has enough money to buy his own equipment, to buy a horse and to campaign at his own expense, should go to Mainz and contact Maréchal Kellermann. He will be admitted into the Emperor's Gendarmes d'Ordonnance.*

Maréchal Kellermann has been given all the powers he needs to organise companies of 80 men and to appoint the officers from among those who have already served and who have the necessary qualities (...)."

As soon as the circular was distributed, the old aristocracy flocked to Mainz to join this new elite corps, the *"Gendarmes d'ordonnance de la Maison de l'Empereur"*. By November, Maréchal Kellermann was able to set up the first two companies (there were to be six); they were organised in the same way as the Chasseurs à Cheval of the Guard. The uniform was designed by General Lacuée and made official in the regulation dated October 1806. It was green with white buttons, without a distinctive colour but with silver striping. The simple horseman looked just like an officer! They were very quickly the envy of the rest of the Guard who thought they were too privileged.

The 135-strong 1st Company was under the command of the Comte de Montmorency-Laval; it was detached from the army and arrived in Berlin on 13 December. The 2nd Company with 150 men was under the orders of the Comte d'Arberg but only joined the army in January 1807. The 3rd and 4th Companies were only operational by April and May 1807. As for the 5th Company, its existence, like that of the Company on Foot, was all too brief.

Indeed only the first three companies took part in the 1807 campaign; the other two stayed in Berlin. First used to pursue Major von Schill's partisans, the Gendarmes d'Ordonnance then fought alongside the Italian division under General Teulié and made a name for themselves in several engagements: their conduct at Kolberg even got their name into the 63rd and 69th *"Bulletins de la Grande Armée"*

At the beginning of April 1807, they reached Marienwerder where they served with the Emperor who reviewed them. Satisfied with their behaviour, he awarded seven Croix of the Légion d'Honneur. Then after several other clashes, they took part in the battle of Friedland, on 14 June.

On 25 June, the peace treaty was signed at Tilsit followed by a lot of festivities during which the troops from both sides fraternised. During a banquet offered to the Russian Imperial Guard by the French Imperial Guard, the Gendarmes d'Ordonnance found themselves among some of their former fellow émigrés. Given the task of hosting the Chevaliers-Gardes, they drank and raised their glasses to *"the former King's Household"*: the aristocracy had not forgotten the Ancien Régime.

This behaviour was not exactly to the liking of the rest of the French Imperial Guard or the senior officers. It was perhaps one of the things that hastened the corps' demise: on 12 July 1807, at Kœnisgberg, the Gendarmes d'Ordonnance paraded in front of Maréchal Bessières who told them they were to be disbanded. The final decree dated the following 23 October showed that the Emperor had not forgotten the services they had rendered: *"The Gendarmes d'Ordonnance companies of our Guard have been disbanded but in order to show them that we are satisfied with what they have done, all the simple Gendarmes who took part in the last campaign may join the Chasseurs, Grenadiers and Dragoons of our Guard"*. As for the rest they had to join the Line or the Velites.

The Gardes d'Honneur

1813… The Russian and Spanish campaigns had taken their toll of the Cavalry of the Imperial Guard. Napoleon had to make up the losses by using one of the Empire's last ressources: conscription. The Emperor created new units led by experienced officers from other regiments stationed in Germany, Italy or Spain; they made up the Young Guard.

As of January 1813, Napoleon who apparently had not learnt anything from his unfortunate experience with the Gendarmes d'Ordonnance, wanted to create a *"six-squadron Regiment of Life Guards"* intended *"to guard the person of the Emperor and the King of Rome"*. In fact in April, he created four Gardes d'Honneur regiments. They were to be recruited among the sons of the nobility and the upper classes, on a volunteer basis. Indeed up until then, most of these young men had got out of conscription by paying for a person to replace them. The decree setting up the unit stipulated that *"the men making up these regiments had to pay for their dress, their equipment and their mounts themselves"*, but that *"they would be paid as though they were Chas-*seurs of the Guard*"*. This last measure was intended to flatter potential volunteers. But they were so few and far between that, faced with such a lack of enthusiasm, the prefects were given orders to conscript the men as a matter of course anyway. This of course led to a good number of deserters. Besides, the replacement system still persisted and a good number of young men from the more modest classes were enrolled in the Gardes d'Honneur and dressed and equipped at the expense of wealthier families who thereby managed to spare their sons the vagaries and uncertainties of military life.

The four regiments got themselves more or less well organised and then started campaigning. They were given their baptism of fire at Leipzig and on 30 October, they charged brilliantly at Hanau to disengage the Grenadiers à Cheval of the Guard. Thanks to illness and desertions, the Gardes d'Honneur took part in the French campaign in greatly reduced numbers. On 13 March 1814, they distinguished themselves at Rheims during a charge in which they captured a whole Russian battery, though not without heavy casualties. On 30 March, at the gates of Paris, the 3rd Gardes d'Honneur made a last charge… It was the end. After the abdication at Fontainebleau, the Gardes d'Honneur disappeared: they returned to their families or they were incorporated into the Royal army. Some of them, the aristocrats, joined the King's Life Guards. At Waterloo, 87 Gardes d'Honneur were still in the Cavalry of the Guard.

Lithuanian Tartars, Krakus and Eclaireurs

The creation of the Lithuanian Tartars, the Krakus and the Eclaireurs all resulted from a tactical need: ever since the Polish campaign in 1806, the French troops were faced with the Cossacks and their particular way of fighting. The Emperor could not rest until he had created light cavalry units armed with lances capable of countering the Cossacks by using the same ways of manœuvring as they did.

The three regiments of Chevau-Légers became lancers from 1809 onwards. The Lithuanian Tartars joined them in 1812. The Krakus were created in 1813 and then the three regiments of Eclaireurs. Details will be given concerning the setting up and the organisation of these various units at the beginning of the chapter dealing with them.

5

The TRUMPETERS

Trumpeter wearing training dress in around 1804, after P. Begnini for Commandant Buquoy's card collection.

Trumpeter wearing reduced campaign dress, serving with the Emperor towards 1806. In these circumstances, he did not wear the natural-coloured canvas over-trousers over the hide breeches.

Trumpeter wearing marching dress during a campaign towards 1806-1808, after P. Begnini for Commandant Bucquoy's set of cards.

Trumpeter wearing full dress about 1807, after P. Begnini in Commandant Bucquoy's set of cards. The red uniform disappeared in around 1806 and was replaced by the sky blue one with crimson distinctives which was more in keeping with the overall dress of the trumpeters in the Cavalry of the Guard.

The TRUMPETERS

Trumpeter wearing interior service dress in around 1807, after P. Begnini. The blue breeches replaced the riding trousers and the second uniform hat without stripes, replaced the bearskin.

Musician wearing full dress in about 1810, after a drawing made from the Alsatian Collections by Commandant Bucquoy who presumed that the sky-blue (and not dark-blue) cover and riding hood had been tailored for the wedding festivities for Napoleon and Marie-Louise.

Trumpeter wearing marching dress in about 1807, after P. Begnini for Commandant Bucquoy. Note the old-style saddle-pack still in use at this period.

Trumpeter wearing full dress during the Hundred Days, after P. Begnini. The dress was unchanged except for the cockades and the Imperial attributes which were replaced by the King's during the First Restoration.

The KETTLEDRUMMER

In the foreground, the kettledrummer according to Plate N° 6 by Rigo. Behind him, the kettledrummer after the set of plates by Noirmont and Marbot. The red coat shows that he is from the beginning of the Empire since the trumpeters were only issued with sky-blue coats in 1807 and one can presume that the kettledrummer's dress changed in the same way, although there is no proof of this. Commandant Bucquoy's set of cards also gives us a kettledrummer after the engravings by Hoffmann: the coat is quite the same as the version in Marbot's book, but with a red collar and a red and blue drum apron edged with three silver stripes. The drummer is mounted on a very dark brown, almost black, horse.

The OFFICERS

As was the custom, the officers wore the same uniform as the troopers but tailored from better cloth. White, the distinctive colour of the Gendarmerie, was replaced by silver. The strapping was yellow, edged with a silver stripe. The silver belt-plate bore a golden grenade. The silver aiglets were worn on the right after 1804. The sabre had a silver shell-shaped guard decorated with a grenade. All the decorations were silver. The sabre-knot was silver.

Officers in social dress, 1804-1815.
On the left, according to Commandant Bucquoy; on the right, after Michel Pétard.

Officer wearing second drill dress in around 1810, after a drawing by P. Begnini. He is wearing an overcoat without epaulettes or aglets and is riding on a leather saddle without cover or hoods.

Officer wearing a coat after a drawing by Commandant Bucquoy who gave an anonymous engraving made in 1805 in Vienna as his source.

The OFFICERS

A pair of captain's epaulettes.

Officer's coat. In the Guard, the aglet was worn on the right-hand side. The ornaments on the turnbacks and the shoulder loops were embroidered with silver.

The arms of General Savary, Duke of Rovigo, Colonel-Commandant of the Elite Gendarmerie of the Imperial Guard.

A pair of Colonel's epaulettes.

Officer wearing full service dress. This dress lasted throughout the Empire, except for the turnbacks. These were first pinned, leaving a blue triangle of the coat's cloth visible; then they were flattened and sewn down to the bottom of the coat-tails.

The uniform worn by General Savary, Colonel-Commandant of the Elite Gendarmerie of the Guard, according to Rigo's Plate N°57 in the *Le Plumet*. His coat was embroidered with silver oak leaves on the collar, lapels and turnbacks. As a Colonel in the Guard, Savary was of Major-General rank and bore that rank's distinctives: a double row of oak leaves on the collar and the sash and the epaulettes were decorated with three stars.

The Gendarmes d'Ordonnance

The Gendarmes d'Ordonnance had to pay for their own equipment and uniforms. Although the dress was simple and rather strict-looking, the equipment on the other hand was very luxurious and, according to Lieutenant de Norvins, cost a packet!

The Shako

This was the 1806 model, made of black felt decorated with a black velvet stripe. The visor was made of leather with silver metal edging. The plate was an all-silver metal lozenge with a stamped, crowned eagle. Contemporary sources show that there were variants. The cord was silver braid with two flounders. The chin strap consisted of silver metal scales. The tricolour cockade was held in place by a double silver loop and a silver button. The whole was surmounted by a white plume.

The Coat

This was a green "à la Chasseur" coat with pointed facings and lapels, just like those worn by the Chasseurs à Cheval of the Guard, but much more austere: there was no distinctive colour. The turnbacks were attached with a button, the pockets were tailored "à la Soubise". The round buttons were silver; flat buttons, with a stamped eagle, might also have been used.

The Aiglet

This was the Guards' model. It was a silver braid cord for the troopers and the officers. Although no document confirms this, it can be supposed that the silver NCO aiglet was mixed with green silk. Although there is controversy over the Gendarmes d'Ordonnance belonging to the Guard, period documentary evidence on the other hand does show that they wore aiglets; but these were sometimes worn on the right, sometimes on the left... it depends on the source.

The Waistcoat

This was tailored "à la Hongroise" and was made of scarlet cashmere, decorated with silver braid and three rows of round silver buttons. For the NCOs, the same can be said as for the aiglets: the braid may have been mixed with green silk.

The Breeches and the Riding Breeches

These were Hungarian-style breeches made of green cloth decorated with a silver stripe down the side seams and two Hungarian knots on the front that were sometimes replaced by a single stripeshaped into an inverted point. The riding breeches or "charivari" were made of green cloth. The inner leg was lined with green cloth or with blackened sheepskin. The sides were fastened with buttons and the stripe was identical to that of the breeches.

Equipment

This comprised the cartridge box and its strap, a musketoon-holder belt and a belt. All this black leather-work was varnished and had silver stitching. Some documents show the leather-work with scarlet stitches. All the buckles were silver-coloured. The cartridge case had a plate like the one on the shako. There was a stamped eagle attached to a pin decorating the front of its strap. The whole was silver-coloured.

Weapons

As the Gendarmes d'Ordonnance were organised like the Chasseurs à Cheval of the Guard, they should have been armed with the 1786-model musketoon but nothing is less certain and the pistol should have been An XIII-model, but no document confirms this.

Harnessing

This was Hungarian-style. The leather was black and the buckles silver. The shabrack was made of green cloth decorated with a silver stripe and scarlet piping. The corners were embroidered with a silver eagle. The portmanteau had silver striping.

The Marks of Rank

The only things to distinguish the officers from the troopers were the one or two silver epaulettes, and the width of the stripes. There are no reliable sources for the senior officers or the NCOs.

The Gendarmes d'Ordonnance

Gendarme d'Ordonnance
in full dress towards 1807,
according to Kolbe.

Gendarme
d'Ordonnance in
full dress towards
1807, according to
Henschel. Note that
the aiglet was worn
on the left and not
on the right.

Gendarme d'Ordonnance
wearing full dress
towards 1807 according
to a plate by H. Boisselier.

Gendarme d'Ordonnance wearing full
dress in around 1807, according to
Noirmont and Marbot. On this plate,
they have given him a sabre belonging
to the Chasseurs à Cheval of the Guard.
Note on the breeches that the silver
stripe has been doubled up where it
ought to be single and the Hungarian-
style knot has been replaced
by an inverted point.

Were the Gendarmes d'Ordonnance
part of the Imperial Guard or not?
This is a controversial point. The
Imperial circular sent to Kellermann
only mentioned the *"Gendarmes
d'Ordonnance of the Emperor"*, but
the decree dated 1 October 1806
showed that *"(...) By its very
institution, this corps will be part
of the Imperial Guard and will have
the same advantages (...)"*. They
were organised like the Chasseurs à
Cheval of the Guard which was
confirmed in a decree dated 12 April
stipulating in its 1st Article that *"The
1st and 2nd Companies of the
Gendarmes d'Ordonnance be
included with regiments of the
Chasseurs à Cheval of the Guard
where pay, accounting, credits and
administration were concerned,
except for the first instalment"*. As
the other companies were not
mentioned, it can indeed be inferred
that only the first two companies
were part of the Imperial Guard.

The Gendarmes d'Ordonnance

Gendarme d'Ordonnance in full dress according to the set from the Alsatian Collections.

Gendarme d'Ordonnance wearing full dress according to the plate by H. Boisselier.

Gendarme d'Ordonnance in full dress according to the Weiland manuscript.

Gendarme officer in full dress according to the Alsatian Collections. The only details which distinguish him from an ordinary gendarme are the epaulette of his rank and the silver stripe on his shako. The stripe on his breeches ought to be wider, but it cannot be seen properly here as it is shown from the front.

NCO Gendarme wearing town dress according to the Alsatian Collections. Strangely enough, the hat does not have a cockade.

Service Dress and Marching Uniforms

Gendarme wearing a coat according to H. Boisselier. This is a greatcoat-cloak with sleeves, in use at the end of the Empire.

Gendarme wearing a cloak according to the Alsatian Collections. He is wearing a grey sleeveless cavalry cloak normally worn at the beginning of the Empire.

Gendarme in marching dress after H. Boisselier.

Gendarme wearing marching dress or the uniform for picket duty for the Emperor, after a drawing by P. Courcelle. Like the coat for the Chasseurs à Cheval of the Guard, the round cloak could be removed and worn by itself.

Gendarme wearing a frock-coat according to the Alsatian Collections. Normally, this coat was only issued to officers and NCOs. However here, this one has neither epaulettes nor stripes of rank. It is possible that simple Gendarmes were issued with them, especially considering their special status (some would have said "privileged") within the Imperial Guard.

The Company on Foot

Gendarme wearing full dress according to the Alsatian Collections. Note the black leather-work with red stripes and the plate on the sabre-holder belt decorated with a grenade.

Gendarmes from the Company on Foot wearing full dress. Note that mounting of the short *sabre-briquet* belonging to the Gendarme seen from behind is silver coloured.

Gendarme wearing an overcoat after H. Boisselier.

Gendarme wearing full dress after Noirmont and Marbot.

"[...] Having noticed that among the proposals which had been made to me, a great number of citizens wanted to campaign on foot, His Majesty kindly granted my request and allowed these young people to be part of a ordnance corps on foot [...]". This Company on Foot was formed at Mainz on 26 December 1806 only to be disbanded on 28 April 1807 since it never reached the required strength. It did not take part in any campaigns. The drawings of the Company on Foot have been made after H. Boisselier's plates, whose own sources were the Carl Collections and the reports from General Lacuée.

15

Trumpeters and Drummers

Trumpeter according to the Boeswilwald Collection of small soldiers in Strasbourg. This uniform is often shown by contemporary illustrators but it is difficult to know how reliable it is, seeing how different it is from the other two. Note the strange colour of the saddlepack.

Drummer in the Company on Foot according to the plate by H. Boisselier

Trumpeter according to the plate by H. Boisselier.

Trumpeter according to Plate N°176 in *Le Plumet* by Rigo. This is the uniform worn on 1 and 2 July 1807, during the parade at Tilsit, held in front of the three Emperors, Alexander I, Frederick-William III and Napoleon.

16

Uniform Items

The aiglet was normally worn on the right but, as seen on the previous pages, the side depended on the sources.

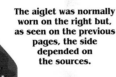

Gendarme d'Ordonnance's "A la Chasseur" coat. Right: a Trumpeter's coat according to Rigo. Left and bottom: the Trooper's coat. This was very simple, without any trimmings. Its only luxuries were the buttons which were silver and the aiglet of the Guard which was silver braid.

Trooper's shako.

Officer's shako.

Shako plates for the Compagnies à Cheval. Top: the classic plate, silver, decorated with a crowned eagle. Centre: a plate with a longer lozenge decorated with a eagle without a crown, after a drawing by L. Fallou published in *La Garde Impériale*. Bottom: a plate cut out in the form of an eagle, after Kolbe.

Hat for the Company on Foot. It was also the hat worn by the Compagnies à Cheval for their second uniform.

Hungarian-style breeches with silver trimmings.

"Charivari" trousers

Hungarian-style waistcoat. It was made of cashmere and the trimmings were made of silver braid.

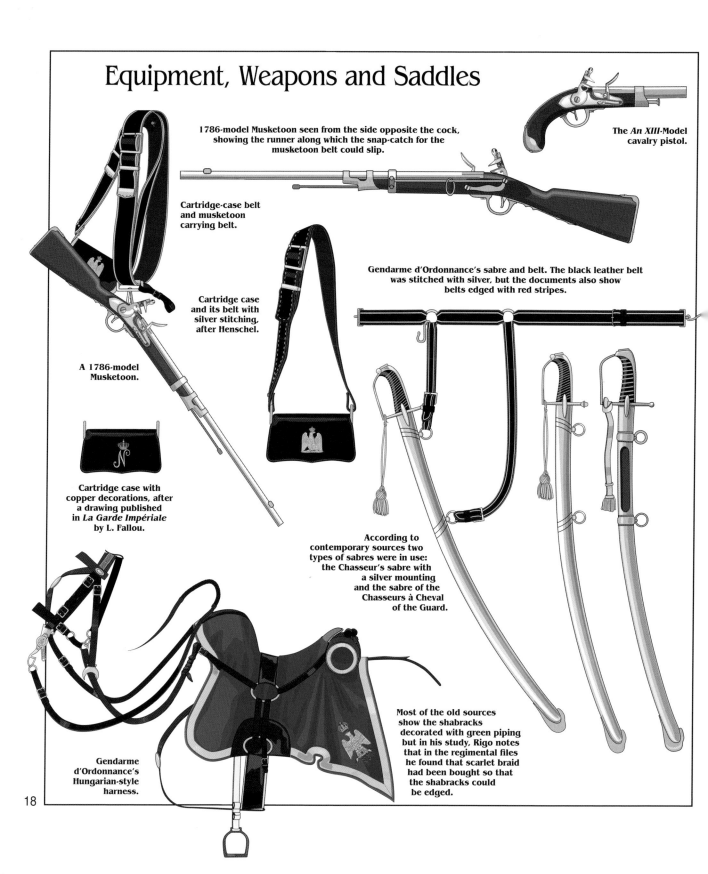

Equipment, Weapons and Saddles

1786-model Musketoon seen from the side opposite the cock, showing the runner along which the snap-catch for the musketoon belt could slip.

The *An XIII*-Model cavalry pistol.

Cartridge-case belt and musketoon carrying belt.

Cartridge case and its belt with silver stitching, after Henschel.

Gendarme d'Ordonnance's sabre and belt. The black leather belt was stitched with silver, but the documents also show belts edged with red stripes.

A 1786-model Musketoon.

Cartridge case with copper decorations, after a drawing published in *La Garde Impériale* by L. Fallou.

According to contemporary sources two types of sabres were in use: the Chasseur's sabre with a silver mounting and the sabre of the Chasseurs à Cheval of the Guard.

Gendarme d'Ordonnance's Hungarian-style harness.

Most of the old sources show the shabracks decorated with green piping but in his study, Rigo notes that in the regimental files he found that scarlet braid had been bought so that the shabracks could be edged.

The Gardes d'Honneur

The decree dated 5 April 1813 gives us a full description of the uniform and the equipment of the Gardes d'Honneur. "(...) *The four regiments will be dressed, equipped and armed in the Hussar fashion (...) The uniform for the four regiments will be the same: the pelisse will be dark green with white flannel lining and black skin on the border, the edge of the collar, the boudin (false pocket) and around the sleeves, together with white cord, braid loops and tresses. The background colour of the dolman will be dark green with scarlet facings and collar; there will also be tresses on the collar, false pockets and facings the same colour as the pelisse. The Hungarian-style breeches will be made of red cloth with white braid. The buttons will be white, the belt crimson and white, and the shako red.*"

After a number of incidents, the regiments were eventually formed. But as far as dress, equipment and weapons were concerned the results were rather catastrophic. Although some of the Guards wore tailor-made uniforms, most of them wore uniforms cut from poor-quality cloth with a wide range of colour shades. The trousers were either too short or too long, or the shakos were too big. In a report dated 13 October 1813, Nansouty wrote: "(...) *These corps are generally badly dressed, badly equipped and badly presented. They also have a lot of bad horses (...).*"

Particular details concerning important points of dress, equipment and weapons are described below.

The Shako

This was more bulky than the regulation 1812 model. Made out of strong cardboard or leather, it was covered with red cloth. There was a white thread braid stripe around the upper circumference. It had a silver brass plate as required by the 1812 regulations comprising an eagle standing on a base; the regimental number was cut out of this base. The visor was circled with silver metal. The chin strap consisted of a small silver chain sewn on to a strip of red cloth. The cord was plaited with two white thread flounders. In the Gardes d'Honneur, the flounders were worn on the left.

The plume was green. The colour of the tip was the distinctive: red for the 1st Regiment, sky blue for the 2nd, yellow for the 3rd and white for the 4th. There was a pompom the same colour as the squadron at the base of the plume. With the second uniform, the Gardes d'Honneur wore a pompom with a pendant the same colour as the regimental distinctive.

The Dolman, Pelisse and Sash

These were the same models as those used by the Hussar regiments, but they were cut shorter than at the beginning of the Empire, thus following the fashion of the times and wearing the waist very high. The eighteen white tresses held five rows of large, medium and small, round silver buttons. The sash-belt had crimson cords with white loops.

The Sabretache

This was made very simply from varnished black leather and bore a crowned eagle over the regimental number. These ornaments were cut out of red silver copper.

Weapons

In theory, the troopers were to have an *An-XI* light cavalry sabre, an *An-XIII* cavalry musketoon and a pair of *An-XIII* model pistols. However because supplying them was difficult, very few Gardes received a full set of weapons.

The Non-Commissioned Officers and Officers

The shako cord, together with the braid on the dolman, the pelisse and the waistcoat should have been silver mixed with green. But documents show that the regulations were not respected very often.

The officers wore the same uniform as the troopers, but their cloth was finer. The shako stripes and the cord with the flounders were silver. They sometimes wore a colback with a scarlet pendant with silver piping and towards the end of the Empire, the *shako-rouleau* (a taller, more cylindrical shako). All the trimmings on the dolman, the pelisse, the waistcoat and the breeches were silver. The equipment, which on the whole was of good quality, was made of red or green leather, and sometimes had fancy striping. The sabretaches were covered with cloth and decorated with a stripe; the ornaments were embroidered with silver, or sometimes with gold.

The 1ˢᵗ Gardes d'Honneur Regiment

Were the Gardes d'Honneur really part of the Imperial Guard? It is true that Article 6 of the decree dated 5 April 1813 stipulated that: *"they would have the pay of the Chasseurs of the Garde"*; moreover, they wore the same straight "stick" embroidery on their uniforms and the same aiglet as the Guard. All these elements would seem to indicate that they belonged to the Guard. But on 25 April the Minister Director of the War Administration announced that *"under the present system of financing, the Gardes d'Honneur regiments will be assimilated with the Line Corps."* Although the Emperor wanted them to serve him, at the Battle of Leipzig for example and *"clearly intended to incorporate them into the Imperial Guard"*, he never actually decided once and for all to make it official.

Sabretache belonging to the 1ˢᵗ Regiment of the Gardes d'Honneur.

Garde d'Honneur wearing full dress according to the Musée de l'Armée Collections.

Garde wearing full dress in about 1813, after the plate by Martinet. If the green of the gloves was not the result of a colour defect in the engraving, it shows that this Garde did want to be "fashionable".

Garde wearing full dress according to a drawing of Dutch origin. Note that the border of the pelisse which is most likely white lamb's wool. This sort of extravagance is very rarely seen in the documents devoted to the Gardes d'Honneur.

The 1st Gardes d'Honneur Regiment

Garde according to the plates
by Martinet in about 1814. This is
another interpretation of the Gardes
d'Honneur uniform. The fact that
the plume is entirely white suggests
that this is a uniform worn during
the Hundred Days or even after
the collapse of the Empire.

Garde wearing town dress after
an aquarelle by L. Rousselot.
It seems that social dress was
rarely worn by the troopers.

Garde d'Honneur wearing his pelisse.
A contemporary anecdote tells how some Gardes
were not acquainted with the Hussar-style dress
and fastened their sash-belt over
the pelisse they were wearing!

The 1ˢᵗ Gardes d'Honneur Regiment

Garde wearing drill fatigues with a stable jacket after an aquarelle by L. Rousselot

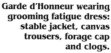

Garde d'Honneur wearing grooming fatigue dress: stable jacket, canvas trousers, forage cap and clogs.

Garde wearing campaign dress. Covered with its black oil-cloth, the shako is surmounted by the pompom with a pendant the same colour as the regiment. Fighting must be just around the corner as this trooper is wearing his coat saltire-wise over his shoulder to protect him from sabre blows or lance thrusts.

Groom assigned to the Gardes d'Honneur to look after their horses. The wealthier Gardes asked permission to take a servant with them. This privilege was granted by decree and must have caused a certain amount of jealousy in the Old Guard. Judge for yourself: *"A groom called a Tartare will be assigned to every two mounted Gardes d'Honneur (...) Each Tartare will groom the horses of two gardes d'Honneur as well as his own (...)"* And yes, you did read correctly: the decree does not mention officers in particular. It concerns simple troopers!

The 1st Regiment Trumpeters

Theoretically, the Trumpeters in the four Gardes d'Honneur regiments ought to have worn the "Imperial Livery" defined by the 1812 regulations, i.e. dark green dolman and pelisse with seven yellow and green livery stripes on each sleeve. In fact, other uniforms were also worn, with each regiment making a point of being different from the others. C. Blondiau has described the various uniforms worn by the trumpeters in a very well-documented article about the Gardes d'Honneur in N° 47 of *Uniformes* magazine.

Trumpeter from the 1st Regiment, given by C. Blondiau, according to period sources. Note that the buttons and embroidery are gold. The sabretache is covered in cloth and has a gold stripe. The gold eagle and the gold regimental number were cut out of metal.

Trumpeter from the 1st Regiment given by C. Blondiau according to period sources. Note that the striping on the breeches is white mixed with sky blue. All the buttons and the rest of the stripes are gold.

Trumpeter from the 1st Regiment. This must be a variant of the previous uniform, but the Hungarian breeches have been replaced by the "charivari" trousers. This dress was described by Commandant Bucquoy.

The 1st Regiment Officers

The uniform worn by General Count Randon de Pully. He was 63 at the time and was in command of the 1st Regiment at the Versailles depot; General Piquet, the second-in-command, was given command of the war squadrons. As the Colonel Commandant held the rank of Major-General, he therefore wore his Major-General's three stars on his stripes of rank as was the custom in the Guard. Moreover like most senior officers, his uniform has gold buttons and trimmings.

Officer wearing social dress, after an aquarelle by L. Rousselot.

Officer in the 1st Regiment wearing full dress. Note in particular the stripe around the upper circumference of the shako: it is made of black velvet with a string of silver rings resembling that on the shakos of the 1st Eclaireur Regiment of the Guard: he could have been assigned to them at the beginning of the Campaign for France.

Clothing

Shakos belonging to troopers from the four regiments.
Some descriptions mention the fact that the Gardes d'Honneur shakos were bigger than those of other corps. Other sources show shakos which were wider at the top. Moreover some shakos were like those worn by the Rhine Confederation troops. The 4th Regiment shako on the right of the row was worn under the First Restoration as borne out by the completely white plume, and the eagle which has been broken off the plate.

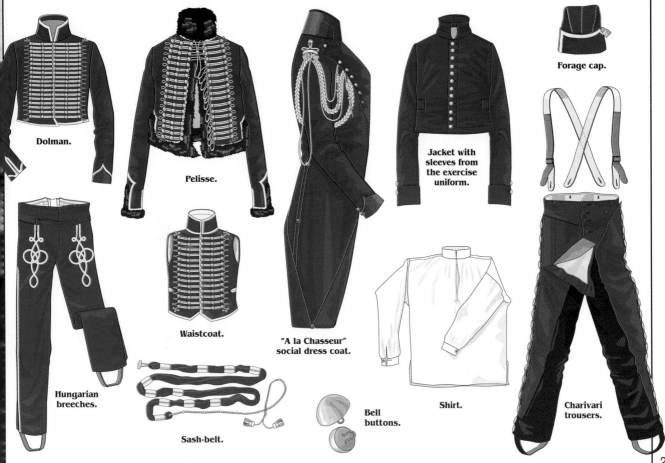

Dolman.

Pelisse.

Jacket with sleeves from the exercise uniform.

Forage cap.

Hungarian breeches.

Waistcoat.

"A la Chasseur" social dress coat.

Sash-belt.

Bell buttons.

Shirt.

Charivari trousers.

Troopers' and Officers' Equipment

The holding belt was attached to the steel slip ring and snap-hook.

Complete light cavalry equipment: cartridge case belt, cartridge case and musketoon-holder belt.

Steel slip ring and hook.

Belt used by the light cavalry. It consisted of three belts doubled over and sewn onto three brass rings. The longest belt was adjustable thanks to a buckle and prong. Small buckles enabled the length of the three sabretache belts and the two sabre belts to be adjusted. The equipment was made of white buffalo hide without any top stitches. Indeed, although the Gardes d'Honneur were paid like the Guard, they nevertheless still came under the Ministry of War, like the troops of the Line. They were therefore issued with standard strappings.

The Hussar type cartridge case was made of blackened leather without any decorations. A small wooden case inside contained the cartridges and small tools for the up-keep of the weapons.

Gardes d'Honneur officer's belt.

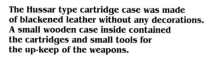

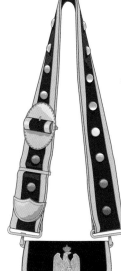

Gardes d'Honneur officer's cartridge case. This is one model among many, since there must have been a host of variants: red, green or black leather; silver or gold buckles and embroidery, with or without eagle.

The officer's sabretaches shown here are only three examples of the wide variety of models which surely existed.

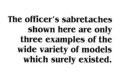

Buckles for fastening an officer's belt.

When wearing campaign uniform, the officers could also carry a black leather sabretache like the troopers' but it was very clearly far better made.

26

Troopers' and Officers' Weapons

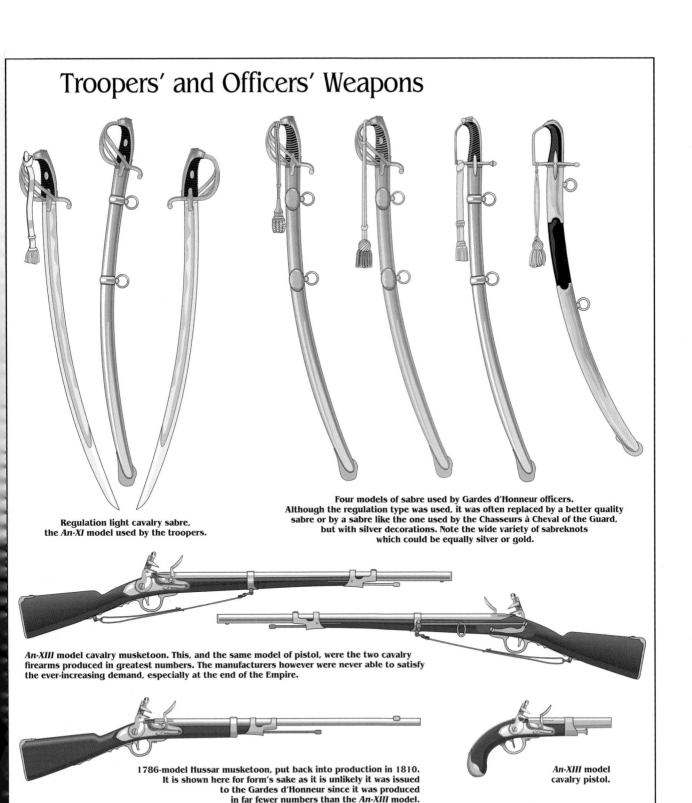

**Regulation light cavalry sabre,
the *An-XI* model used by the troopers.**

**Four models of sabre used by Gardes d'Honneur officers.
Although the regulation type was used, it was often replaced by a better quality
sabre or by a sabre like the one used by the Chasseurs à Cheval of the Guard,
but with silver decorations. Note the wide variety of sabreknots
which could be equally silver or gold.**

An-XIII model cavalry musketoon. This, and the same model of pistol, were the two cavalry
firearms produced in greatest numbers. The manufacturers however were never able to satisfy
the ever-increasing demand, especially at the end of the Empire.

**1786-model Hussar musketoon, put back into production in 1810.
It is shown here for form's sake as it is unlikely it was issued
to the Gardes d'Honneur since it was produced
in far fewer numbers than the *An-XIII* model.**

An-XIII model
cavalry pistol.

27

Troopers' Saddles

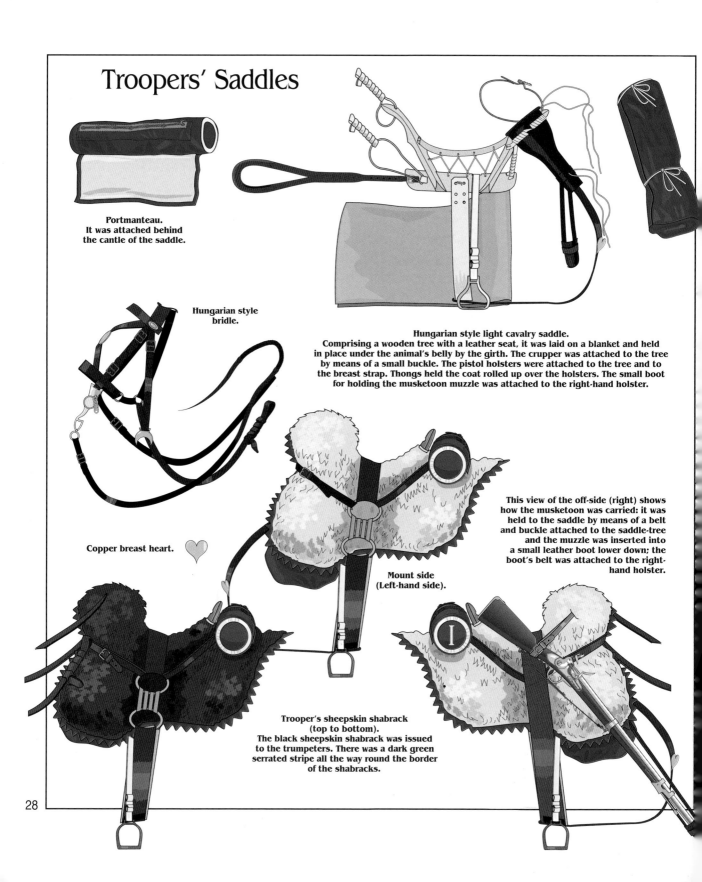

Portmanteau.
It was attached behind
the cantle of the saddle.

**Hungarian style
bridle.**

Hungarian style light cavalry saddle.
Comprising a wooden tree with a leather seat, it was laid on a blanket and held
in place under the animal's belly by the girth. The crupper was attached to the tree
by means of a small buckle. The pistol holsters were attached to the tree and to
the breast strap. Thongs held the coat rolled up over the holsters. The small boot
for holding the musketoon muzzle was attached to the right-hand holster.

Copper breast heart.

This view of the off-side (right) shows
how the musketoon was carried: it was
held to the saddle by means of a belt
and buckle attached to the saddle-tree
and the muzzle was inserted into
a small leather boot lower down; the
boot's belt was attached to the right-
hand holster.

**Mount side
(Left-hand side).**

**Trooper's sheepskin shabrack
(top to bottom).**
The black sheepskin shabrack was issued
to the trumpeters. There was a dark green
serrated stripe all the way round the border
of the shabracks.

Officers' Saddlery

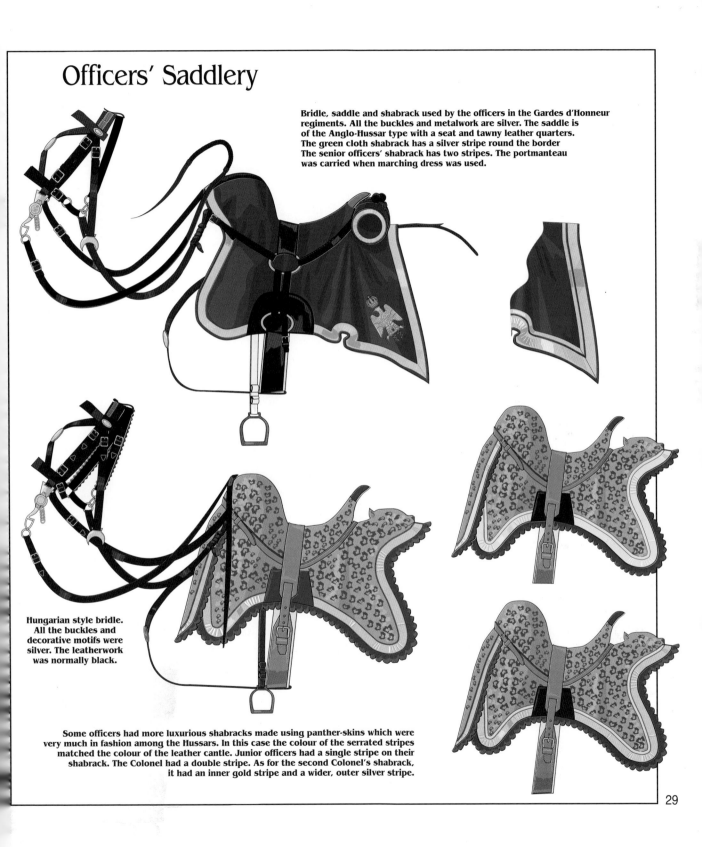

Bridle, saddle and shabrack used by the officers in the Gardes d'Honneur regiments. All the buckles and metalwork are silver. The saddle is of the Anglo-Hussar type with a seat and tawny leather quarters. The green cloth shabrack has a silver stripe round the border The senior officers' shabrack has two stripes. The portmanteau was carried when marching dress was used.

Hungarian style bridle. All the buckles and decorative motifs were silver. The leatherwork was normally black.

Some officers had more luxurious shabracks made using panther-skins which were very much in fashion among the Hussars. In this case the colour of the serrated stripes matched the colour of the leather cantle. Junior officers had a single stripe on their shabrack. The Colonel had a double stripe. As for the second Colonel's shabrack, it had an inner gold stripe and a wider, outer silver stripe.

29

The 2ⁿᵈ Gardes d'Honneur Regiment

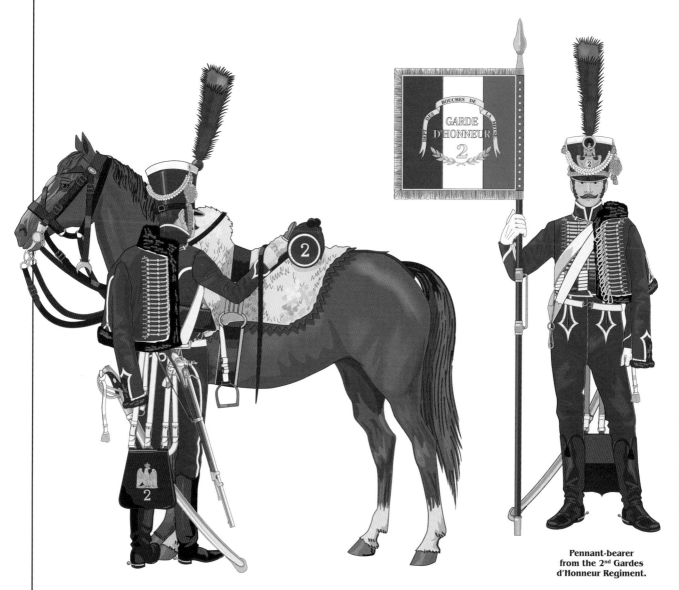

**Garde d'Honneur from the 2ⁿᵈ Regiment
wearing full dress.**

**Pennant-bearer
from the 2ⁿᵈ Gardes
d'Honneur Regiment.**

There is a story about the strange pennant which the Garde shown above, right is holding. The Gardes d'Honneur levied in 1813 in the Bouches-de-la-Meuse (Low Countries), which was a new French *Département* in 1811, had to join the 2ⁿᵈ Regiment which was being formed up. This emblem was made by the wife of the Prefect and was presented to them when they left. But when they reached Metz, General Lepic, the Colonel commanding the regiment, ordered this pennant with its non-regulation motif to be destroyed. An identical pennant has been preserved in the Amsterdam Museum which supposes either that the pennant escaped destruction or that a second example was made after the Dutch Gardes d'Honneur in the 2ⁿᵈ Regiment returned home, as a souvenir of their campaigns.

The 2ⁿᵈ Gardes d'Honneur Regiment

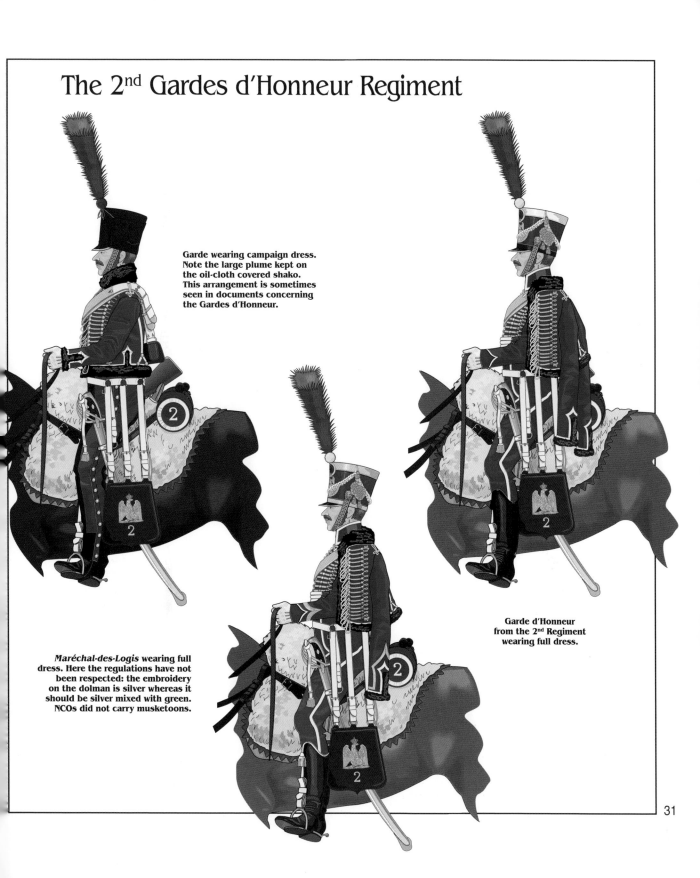

Garde wearing campaign dress. Note the large plume kept on the oil-cloth covered shako. This arrangement is sometimes seen in documents concerning the Gardes d'Honneur.

Maréchal-des-Logis wearing full dress. Here the regulations have not been respected: the embroidery on the dolman is silver whereas it should be silver mixed with green. NCOs did not carry musketoons.

Garde d'Honneur from the 2ⁿᵈ Regiment wearing full dress.

The 2nd Regiment Trumpeters

Trumpeter from the 2nd Regiment wearing campaign dress after an aquarelle by L. Rousselot.

Trumpeter in the 2nd Regiment in full dress according to the 1812 regulations. His dolman and pelisse are decorated with the famous "Imperial Livery" embroidery.

Trumpeter in the 2nd Regiment in full dress, after a drawing by Jack Girbal for Dr. Hourtoulle's collection of plates.

The 3rd Gardes d'Honneur Regiment

Garde from the 3rd Regiment wearing full dress, according to the engravings by A. Martinet. The green gloves and the shape of the sheepskin shabrack are the same as those worn by the trooper in the 1st Regiment.

Garde wearing campaign dress. The shako covered with its protective oil-cloth is has a pompom with a pendant the same colour as the regimental distinctive.

Garde during the Campaign for France. Note that the two plaits on the shako cord are worn on the front. This arrangement seems to have been specific to the 3rd Regiment as it is sometimes to be found in documents about the regiment.

The 3rd Regiment Trumpeters

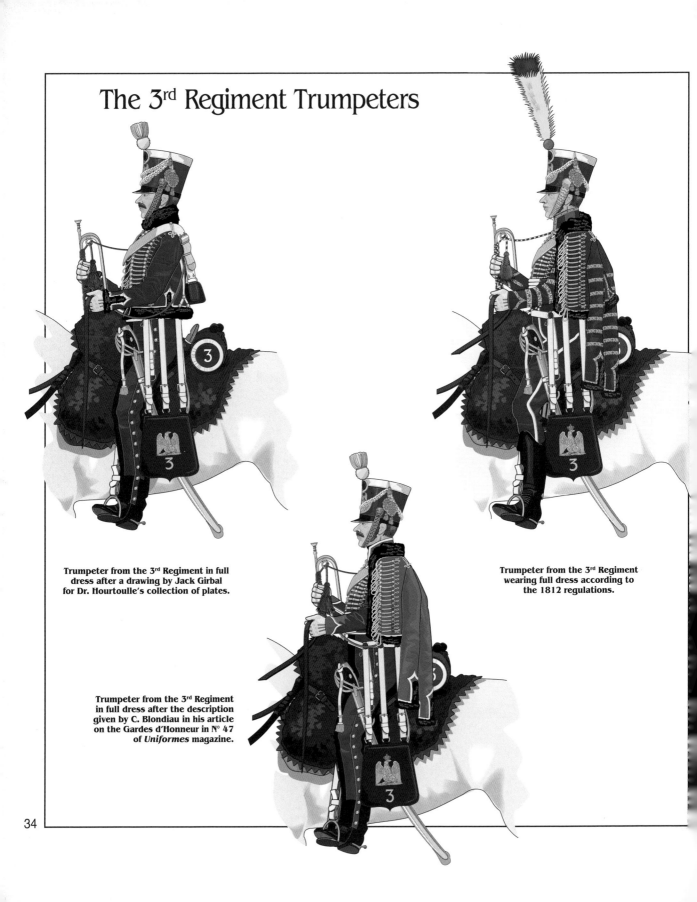

Trumpeter from the 3rd Regiment in full dress after a drawing by Jack Girbal for Dr. Hourtoulle's collection of plates.

Trumpeter from the 3rd Regiment in full dress after the description given by C. Blondiau in his article on the Gardes d'Honneur in N° 47 of *Uniformes* magazine.

Trumpeter from the 3rd Regiment wearing full dress according to the 1812 regulations.

The 3rd Regiment Officers

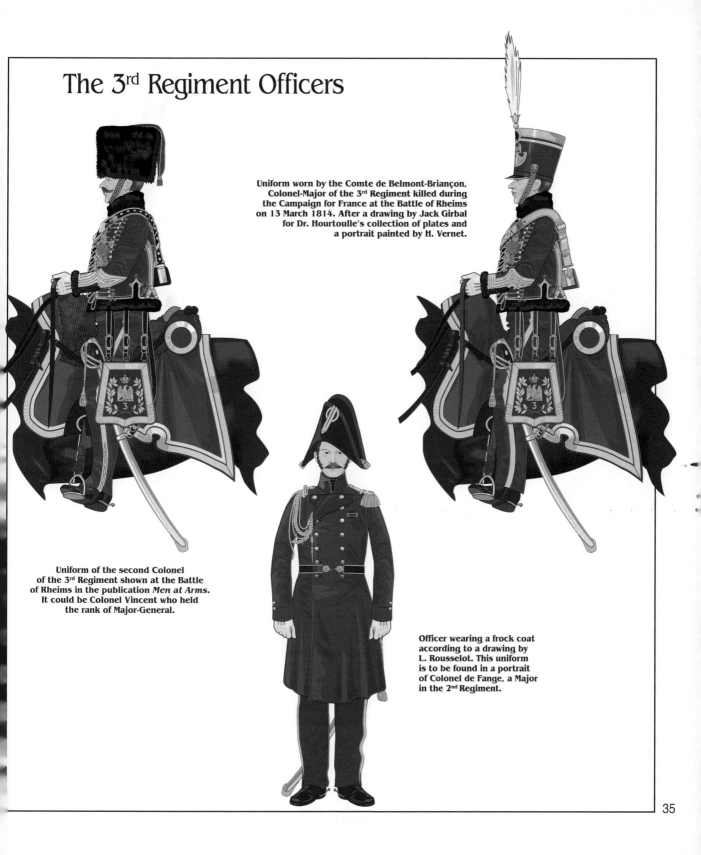

Uniform worn by the Comte de Belmont-Briançon,
Colonel-Major of the 3rd Regiment killed during
the Campaign for France at the Battle of Rheims
on 13 March 1814. After a drawing by Jack Girbal
for Dr. Hourtoulle's collection of plates and
a portrait painted by H. Vernet.

Uniform of the second Colonel
of the 3rd Regiment shown at the Battle
of Rheims in the publication *Men at Arms*.
It could be Colonel Vincent who held
the rank of Major-General.

Officer wearing a frock coat
according to a drawing by
L. Rousselot. This uniform
is to be found in a portrait
of Colonel de Fange, a Major
in the 2nd Regiment.

The 4th Gardes d'Honneur Regiment

Garde d'Honneur from the 4th Regiment at the Battle of Leipzig, after a gouache by an anonymous eye-witness, preserved at the Marmottan Museum in Paris. As he was in service with the Emperor, he is wearing escort dress. There are some oddities however. He is using a green cloth shabrack with a red stripe and a sheepskin seat, not to mention the rectangular portmanteau! Perhaps the artist was not able to interpret what he saw correctly…

Maréchal-des-Logis Chef in social dress. This reconstitution is based on the articles of the regulations concerning NCOs, and an aiglet preserved in the collections of the Musée de l'Armée.

NCO from the 4th regiment wearing full dress, after the collections in the Musée de l'Empéri. Here the silver embroidery mixed with green respects the regulations which is not the case of the *Brigadier* shown opposite, right.

Brigadier from the 4th Regiment in full dress, after a period miniature. As for the black velvet stripe decorated with a string of silver rings, see our remark about the officer in the 1st Regiment, page 24.

36

The 4ᵗʰ Regiment Trumpeters

Trumpeter from the 4ᵗʰ Regiment wearing campaign dress in 1814. Note the mix of colours in the trimmings which are partly gold and partly silver.

Trumpeter from the 4ᵗʰ regiment in full dress, after R. Knötel. His uniform is the same as that of the trumpeter in the 2ⁿᵈ Regiment except for the colour of the tip of the plume.

Trumpeter from the 4ᵗʰ Regiment in full dress, after the gouache mentioned on the previous page. The two trumpeters wearing full dress seen in that picture are each wearing a red dolman with white tresses, a pelisse edged with white lambskin and red trousers with a yellow stripe. Note the red cloth shabrack with a sheepskin seat and that strange rectangular portmanteau.

The 4ᵗʰ Regiment Officers

Officer from the 4ᵗʰ Regiment wearing campaign dress. Towards the end of the Empire some officers may have worn the *shako-rouleau*, already used in some of the light cavalry regiments.

Uniform worn by Major-General Bonardi de Saint-Sulpice, the Colonel commanding the 4ᵗʰ Regiment. He is wearing his Major-General's three stars on the stripes of his rank. All the trimmings on his uniform and the harness are gold.

38

The Lithuanian Tartars

All one has to do is read the Emperor's letters during the 1807 Campaign to understand how much the Cossacks worried him. Here are some extracts, among several others:

"Landsberg, 18 February 1807, to General Duroc (...) Go ahead with the training of six hundred Polish Guards; I would very much like to have them in a month. Speak seriously to the government and to Prince Poniatowski about organising 3 to 4 000 cavalry to counter the Cossacks (...).

Liebstadt, 20 February 1807, to General Duroc (...) I have been informed that 900 Polish cavalry have reached Osterode; they will be my Cossacks. It would be a great help to the army if there were 3 or 4 000 of them (...)".

During the campaign, Napoleon did not rest until he had raised some Polish cavalry regiments into the Line capable of fighting the Cossacks. But he also thought of his Guard. In March 1807 he created the 1st Chevau-Légers Regiment, followed by another in September 1810 then a third in July 1812.

In June 1812, Imperial troops occupied Lithuania. General van Hogendorp, Governor-General and aide-de-camp to Napoleon suggested levying a regiment from among the Muslim Tartars settled in Lithuania since the Middle Ages. Indeed the idea was put forward to him by Major Mustapha Mura Achmatovicz who proposed to recruit the unit himself, on the condition that it be part of the Imperial Guard. Since cavalry was needed to counter the Cossack threat, Napoleon accepted.

But the recruitment was not up to expectations and only one squadron was raised in October 1812. In December the same year the Lithuanian Tartars were almost wiped out at Vilna trying to protect the French troops' retreat. Achmatovicz was killed. The squadron's thirty survivors got through to the French lines at Posen led by Captain Samuel Hurzan Ulan.

In 1813, Ulan was allowed to raise a new Tartar regiment from among Russian prisoners, but in vain. He only succeeded in recruiting fifteen or so men.

In March 1813, Maréchal Bessières decided to incorporate what remained of the Tartar squadron, fifty men or so, into the remnants of the 3rd Regiment of Lithuanian Chevau-Légers of the Guard crushed at Slomin in October 1812 (See Vol. III of the *Garde*). In the end, in December 1813, the Lithuanian Tartars and Chevau-Légers were attached to the 1st Polish Chevau-Léger Regiment of the Guard, though still serving as distinct units. Thus they took part in the German campaign.

When the Cavalry of the Guard was reorganised at the end of 1813, the Tartars, numbering scarcely forty troopers, were used as *Eclaireurs-Lanciers* and took part in the whole of the Campaign for France.

In April 1814 when Napoleon abdicated for the first time, the forty survivors still under Captain Samuel Hurrian Ulan, were released from their oath. They returned to Lithuania with part of the 1st Chevau-Légers Regiment of the Guard under General Krasinski who rather ironically put the regiment at the disposal of the Tsar...

Uniform and Weapons

The oriental origin of these Muslim Tartars was reflected in their uniforms which were very similar to the Mamelukes' on a lot of points: waistcoats with or without sleeves, baggy trousers taken in at the ankle, wide sash-belt, hat surrounded by a turban, etc. The cut of some of the trousers does however reveal a certain Russian, even Cossack influence. Islamic symbolism was present in the crescent decorating the hat and by some of the lance pennants which were half-green and half-white.

The weapons were also oriental: Turkish-style scimitars, daggers, pistols (very likely the Caucasian type), and lances.

When the squadron was first set up, the colour and the ornamentation of the uniforms must have been very varied but after April 1813, as reorganisation and re-equipment got under way, more conventional equipment and weapons were issued to the Lithuanian Tartars who nonetheless managed to keep their ever so characteristic appearance. Some items of their uniforms were even made by Parisian tailors: after all, they did belong to the Guard!

The Lithuanian Tartars

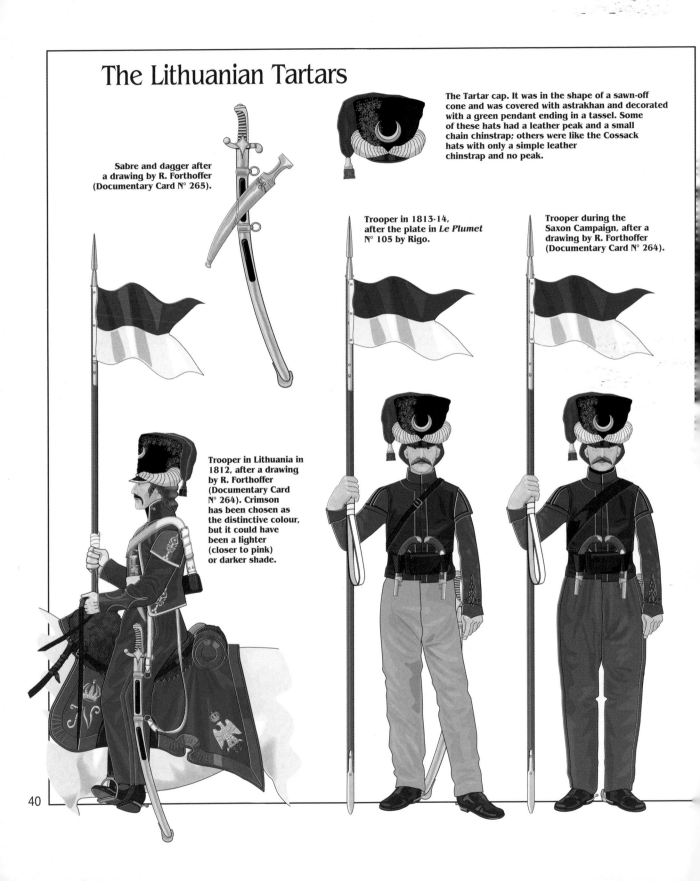

Sabre and dagger after a drawing by R. Forthoffer (Documentary Card N° 265).

The Tartar cap. It was in the shape of a sawn-off cone and was covered with astrakhan and decorated with a green pendant ending in a tassel. Some of these hats had a leather peak and a small chain chinstrap; others were like the Cossack hats with only a simple leather chinstrap and no peak.

Trooper in 1813-14, after the plate in *Le Plumet* N° 105 by Rigo.

Trooper during the Saxon Campaign, after a drawing by R. Forthoffer (Documentary Card N° 264).

Trooper in Lithuania in 1812, after a drawing by R. Forthoffer (Documentary Card N° 264). Crimson has been chosen as the distinctive colour, but it could have been a lighter (closer to pink) or darker shade.

40

The Lithuanian Tartars

Lithuanian Tartar fanion, after a drawing by R. Forthoffer (Documentary Card N° 265). The word "standard" does not seem appropriate since this unit was attached to a regiment of the Guard.

Note the variety of the saddles: apart from the Hungarian style shabracks decorated like the Chevau-Légers', the Tartars used saddlecloths cut in the Polish or Prussian manner.

Trooper in 1813, after a drawing by R. Forthoffer (Documentary Card N° 265).

Trooper in 1813, after a drawing by R. Forthoffer (Documentary Card N° 265).

NCO wearing a greatcoat with a round cloak, according to a drawing by R. Forthoffer (Documentary Card N° 264). Note that the stripes *(which are apparently the equivalent of the French Maréchal-des-Logis Chef)* have been sewn on the sleeves of the coat. This was an arrangement which the other regiments of the Guard did not use.

The Lithuanian Tartars: the Trumpeters

Three Lithuanian Tartar Trumpeters, noted by R. Forthoffer after the Marckolsheim Manuscript.

The two trumpeters, on the left and in the centre, are probably from 1812 and were seen in Lithuania. It is our opinion that it was more likely to have been in 1813, in Germany, since the two trumpeters are wearing belts issued to the Chevau-Légers of the Guard and are carrying an *An-XI* model sabre. It was indeed in March 1813 that the Lithuanian Tartars were incorporated into the 3rd Chevau-Légers Lanciers of the Guard and they must therefore have been issued with the same equipment and weapons following on the April re-organistion.

The character on the right is a *Brigadier-Trompette*, according to his stripes. He could be dated December 1813 since he is wearing the sky-blue and crimson uniform, the distinctive colours of the Trumpeters in the 1st Regiment of Polish Chevau-Légers of the Guard into which the Lithuanian Tartars were incorporated at the time. Moreover, his silver instrument is the same as the ones used by the trumpeters from the 1st Regiment and he is armed with an *An-XI* model sabre and a pair of cavalry pistols. The three trumpeters are wearing "à la Turque" trousers similar to those worn by the Mamelukes. The same can be said of the boots.

The Lithuanian Tartars: the Officers

Officer according to
a drawing by R. Forthoffer
(Documentary card N° 264).
The author indicated that
the source was Polish.

Officer after a plate in the Noirmont
and Marbot Collection. It is the only
picture of an officer wearing the
epaulettes of his rank. Note the
Cossack-style hat.

Officer at the Battle of Leipzig, 1813,
after the plate in *Le Plumet* N° 228
by Rigo. He looks much more like a
Mameluke officer. It is not absolutely
certain how the Lithuanian Tartar
officers' uniform was cut. After all,
there were only three of them:
a Captain and two Lieutenants.

The Polish Krakus

December 1812: the remnants of the Grande Armée reached Poland and Prussia with the Russians hard on their heels. Napoleon tried to reorganise his army from Paris whilst Prince Poniatowski organised resistance to the Allies. A levy *en masse* among the nobles and the sons of landowners raised only 4 000 men for the Duchy of Warsaw cavalry because there weren't enough army horses.

On 10 January 1813, it was decided to recruit among the peasants, to be equipped at their village's and local lord's expense. But this new cavalry soon turned out to be unusable in the front line because the nobles commanding it had no military experience and because the small farming horses were quite unsuited to fighting; so most of the men were put into the infantry. Those remaining, the more determined ones, made up a light cavalry regiment, the "Krakus", a popular name for the peasants from the Krakov voyevoda (province).

These horsemen were intrepid but quite unable to manœuvre in the normal way, so they were given basic training. They were to be used for fighting Cossacks, using the same tactics: fighting in the vanguard and harassment. These tasks turned out to suit them particularly well. With the 14th Polish Cavalry Regiment (cuirassiers), they formed the vanguard of Prince Poniatowski's VIII Corps and got their baptism of fire on 17 August 1813. They took part in the German campaign and achieved a number of successes like capturing the Grekov Cossacks' flag on 9 September 1813 at Strahwalde.

On 25 September at Zittau, the Emperor saw the Krakus for the first time. At first he was amused by their horses' small size and lack of bearing but when their commanding officer, General Uminski told him about their feats of arms, he wanted them to parade. Their deft and rapid manœuvres impressed him and he declared to Caulaincourt: *"Here are men who can teach the Cossacks a lesson or two and even capture their flags!"* Then turning to Poniatowski, he said: *"I've just reviewed your pigmy cavalry, I want 3000 of them!"*

The Krakus charged at Leipzig, then at Wachau, on 16 October, where they routed a Cossack Guard regiment. But the fighting during this campaign thinned their ranks out and the remnants returned to France to take part in the 1814 Campaign alongside the Chevau-Légers of the Guard. They charged for the last time on 27 March 1814, at Claye (Seine-et-Marne) and returned to Poland after the first abdication.

Some readers may be surprised to see the Krakus being dealt with in this book on the cavalry of the Imperial Guard since they were never actually part of it. They most certainly deserved this honour because of their feats of arms and this is why we were anxious to pay them homage by mentioning them here, along with their fellow Poles of the 1st Regiment of Chevau-Légers of the Guard.

Uniforms, equipment and weapons

The most characteristic feature of the Krakus' uniform was their hat, the "krakuska". This cap was the traditional element of the Krakov voyevoda peasant's festive dress. It was the origin of the Polish Lancers' shapska and all Polish army head dresses up until the present day. Made of crimson cloth, the krakuska had a square crown and the base was surrounded by a black lambskin headband.

Another just as characteristic type of head dress was used in 1814: this was a crimson cloth cap in the shape of a melon with the sides underlined by Russian braid and a tassel on the top. These trimmings were white for the troopers and silver for the officers. The left-hand side was decorated with a Polish cockade and a little white plume.

The drawings on the following pages show us that, in general, the krakus' uniform was very similar to that of their sworn enemies, the Cossacks. Like them they were armed with a lance and a sabre; and the only firearm they used was the pistol. Their saddle was less sophisticated than the other regiments and their equipment was reduced to the bare minimum: no cartridge box or pouch, but individual cylindrical metal cartridge cases worn on the chest.

The Polish Krakus

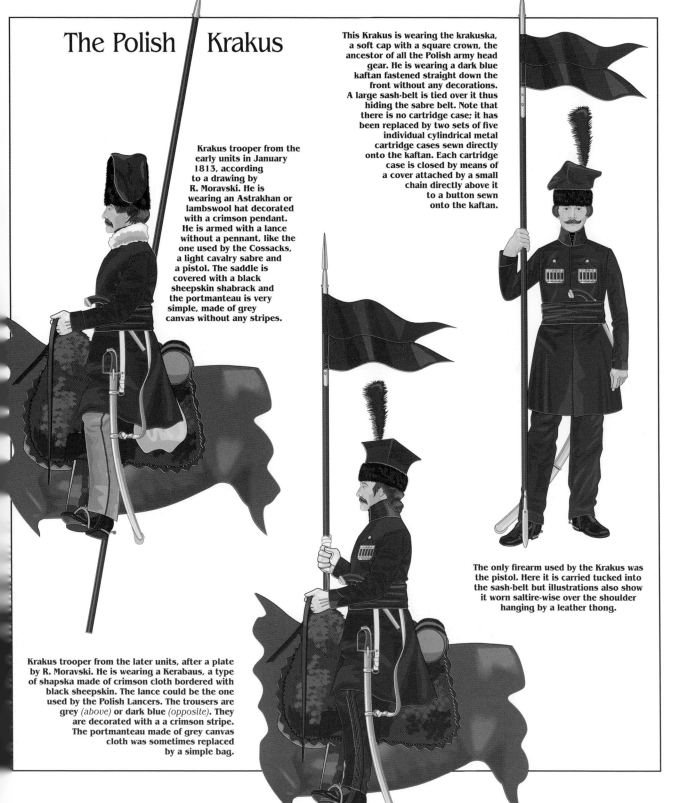

This Krakus is wearing the krakuska, a soft cap with a square crown, the ancestor of all the Polish army head gear. He is wearing a dark blue kaftan fastened straight down the front without any decorations. A large sash-belt is tied over it thus hiding the sabre belt. Note that there is no cartridge case; it has been replaced by two sets of five individual cylindrical metal cartridge cases sewn directly onto the kaftan. Each cartridge case is closed by means of a cover attached by a small chain directly above it to a button sewn onto the kaftan.

Krakus trooper from the early units in January 1813, according to a drawing by R. Moravski. He is wearing an Astrakhan or lambswool hat decorated with a crimson pendant. He is armed with a lance without a pennant, like the one used by the Cossacks, a light cavalry sabre and a pistol. The saddle is covered with a black sheepskin shabrack and the portmanteau is very simple, made of grey canvas without any stripes.

The only firearm used by the Krakus was the pistol. Here it is carried tucked into the sash-belt but illustrations also show it worn saltire-wise over the shoulder hanging by a leather thong.

Krakus trooper from the later units, after a plate by R. Moravski. He is wearing a Kerabaus, a type of shapska made of crimson cloth bordered with black sheepskin. The lance could be the one used by the Polish Lancers. The trousers are grey (*above*) or dark blue (*opposite*). They are decorated with a a crimson stripe. The portmanteau made of grey canvas cloth was sometimes replaced by a simple bag.

45

The Polish Krakus: the Officers

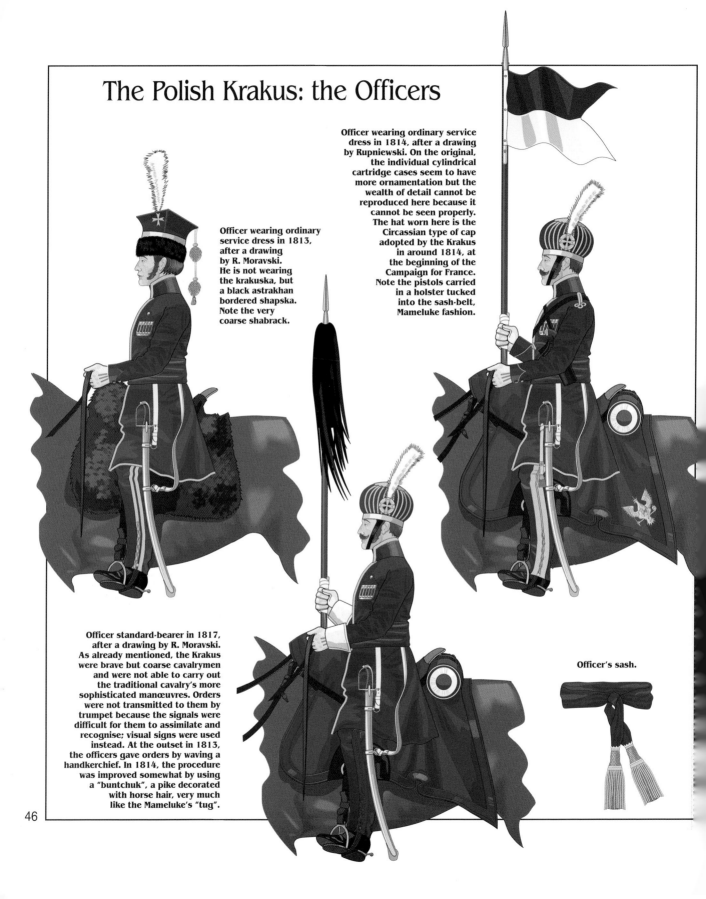

Officer wearing ordinary service dress in 1813, after a drawing by R. Moravski. He is not wearing the krakuska, but a black astrakhan bordered shapska. Note the very coarse shabrack.

Officer wearing ordinary service dress in 1814, after a drawing by Rupniewski. On the original, the individual cylindrical cartridge cases seem to have more ornamentation but the wealth of detail cannot be reproduced here because it cannot be seen properly. The hat worn here is the Circassian type of cap adopted by the Krakus in around 1814, at the beginning of the Campaign for France. Note the pistols carried in a holster tucked into the sash-belt, Mameluke fashion.

Officer standard-bearer in 1817, after a drawing by R. Moravski. As already mentioned, the Krakus were brave but coarse cavalrymen and were not able to carry out the traditional cavalry's more sophisticated manœuvres. Orders were not transmitted to them by trumpet because the signals were difficult for them to assimilate and recognise; visual signs were used instead. At the outset in 1813, the officers gave orders by waving a handkerchief. In 1814, the procedure was improved somewhat by using a "buntchuk", a pike decorated with horse hair, very much like the Mameluke's "tug".

Officer's sash.

The Polish Krakus: the Officers

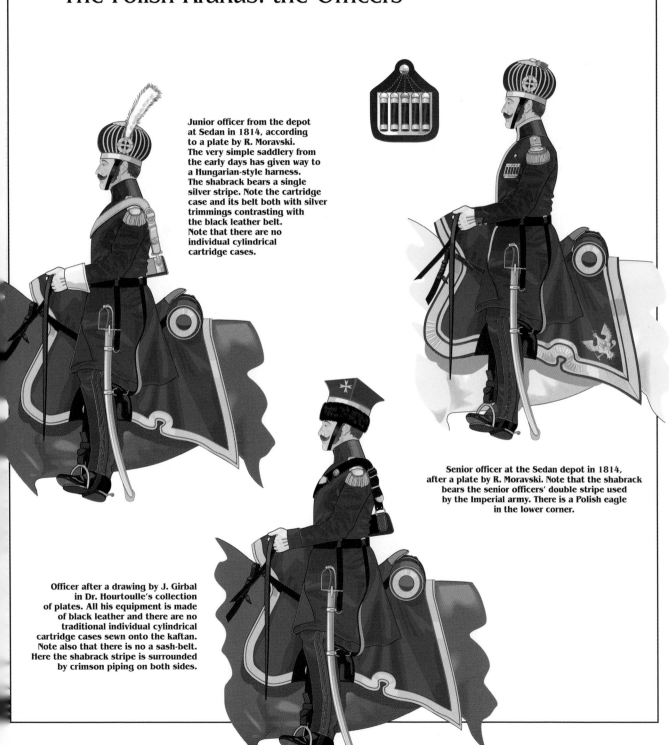

Junior officer from the depot at Sedan in 1814, according to a plate by R. Moravski. The very simple saddlery from the early days has given way to a Hungarian-style harness. The shabrack bears a single silver stripe. Note the cartridge case and its belt both with silver trimmings contrasting with the black leather belt. Note that there are no individual cylindrical cartridge cases.

Senior officer at the Sedan depot in 1814, after a plate by R. Moravski. Note that the shabrack bears the senior officers' double stripe used by the Imperial army. There is a Polish eagle in the lower corner.

Officer after a drawing by J. Girbal in Dr. Hourtoulle's collection of plates. All his equipment is made of black leather and there are no traditional individual cylindrical cartridge cases sewn onto the kaftan. Note also that there is no a sash-belt. Here the shabrack stripe is surrounded by crimson piping on both sides.

The 1ˢᵗ Eclaireur Regiment

On 4 and 9 December 1813, two decrees gave the new composition of the Cavalry of the Guard and ordered the creation of three Eclaireur (Scout) regiments with four 250-men squadrons each. Still intent on creating units capable of countering the Cossacks, the Emperor had the Eclaireurs armed with lances. Each regiment was assigned to a corps of the Guard: the 1ˢᵗ Eclaireurs to the Grenadiers à Cheval, the 2ⁿᵈ to the Dragoons, the 3ʳᵈ to the 1ˢᵗ Chevau-Légers Lancers. Half of the regiments were expected to be ready for 1 January 1814, the rest by 30 January.

Colonel Testot-Ferry of the Dragoons of the Guard was entrusted with the organisation of the 1ˢᵗ Eclaireurs Regiment. The men were raised from the 1st, 3ʳᵈ and 4ᵗʰ Gardes d'Honneur; the 2ⁿᵈ Regiment could not supply any men because it was blockaded in Mainz. The first two squadrons, in the Old Guard, were therefore made up with troopers from the Guard and the Line. The other two squadrons, in the Young Guard, were raised with conscripts and troopers from the Line. All the officers and NCOs came from the Guard.

The Eclaireurs joined the army by detachments to swell the ranks of the cavalry and fought until the capitulation in Paris. They were dismissed when Napoleon abdicated the first time.

The Uniform of the 1ˢᵗ Eclaireur Regiment

The Shako

This was black and cylindrical, and according to contemporary pictures, it seems to have been shorter than the Hussars'shako-rouleau. A black velvet stripe with a string of scarlet rings surrounded its upper circumference. The front was decorated with a white metal eagle under a tricolour cockade. The chin strap, held in place by two lion's head clasps, consisted of a small chain mounted on a leather strip. The visor had a white metal edge. In full dress, a scarlet plume with a black base surmounted the shako. This headdress was common to both Old and Young Guard squadrons.

The Coat

The Old Guard squadrons wore a dark green pelisse ornamented with white tresses and round white metal buttons. Dolmans and Hungarian breeches were scarcely used. The Young Guard squadrons wore a dark green short-tailed coat *(habit-veste)*, fastened down the front with 9 round white metal buttons. The collar, the facings, the turnbacks and the edges of the shoulder flaps were scarlet.

Trousers

These were very full, made of grey cloth and decorated with a scarlet stripe down the leg; they fastened at the bottom of the leg with 8 buttons. There was blackened calfskin lining between the legs ending in a small band on each leg. This was the model used by most of the cavalry corps in the Guard campaigning at the end of the Empire.

Main Equipment

For all the squadrons, this comprised a cartridge case, its shoulder strap and a musketoon-holder strap like those used by the light cavalry of the Line. The strapping was not stitched.

In theory, the Old Guard squadrons wore a belt with sabretache straps, but apparently not all the troopers received this. The Young Guard squadrons were equipped with the belt used by the Chasseurs à Cheval of the Line.

Weapons

Lancer ranks were armed with an 1812-model lance and a *An-XIII*-model pistol hanging from the musketoon-holder strap; Carabinier ranks were armed with the *An-XIII*-model musketoon. Everybody was issued with an *An-XI*-model light cavalry sabre.

Saddlery

The different sources consulted reveal that two types of saddles were used: the classic Hungarian-style saddle covered with a white or scarlet striped shabrack, and a lighter Hungarian leather saddle with panels just placed on a grey blanket.

Given the situation, the latter was most probably used because of concern over simplification and reducing costs. For the same reasons, the head harness was also simplified, but it was not in general use throughout the regiment.

48

The 1ˢᵗ Regiment of Eclaireurs: Old Guard

Eclaireur from the 1ˢᵗ Regiment wearing full dress, after the collection by Valmont and taken up in a study by H. Boisselier. From what he is wearing, this trooper comes from a Gardes d'Honneur regiment.

Brigadier in full dress, after a plate by Rigo in the *Le Plumet* U34. This is in April 1814 and the regiment had not yet been disbanded, but this *Brigadier* does show where his political sympathies lie... with the Bourbons.

Eclaireur from the 1ˢᵗ Regiment wearing full dress, seen from the mount side *(right)* and the offside *(left)*, after an aquarelle by Lucien Rousselot. He is an Eclaireur in the 1ˢᵗ rank: he is armed with a lance and a pistol hanging from the strap normally used for the musketoon. Note the very simplified saddlery consisting of a saddle placed on a blanket.

1st Eclaireur Regiment: Old Guard Squadrons

Eclaireur wearing full-dress, according to the plates by Noirmont and Marbot. The uniform is close to that of the Gardes d'Honneur though the shako plate and the yellow copper chin straps do seem strange.

Eclaireur from the 1st Regiment wearing a greatcoat.

This 1st Eclaireur NCO has most certainly come from a Gardes d'Honneur regiment: he has kept his dolman and pelisse whose tresses are mixed with silver and green silk thread.

Eclaireur wearing full dress, according to the work by Lienhart and Humbert. This study was made after the plates by Noirmont and Marbot and shows the differences in uniform details although they have kept the shako plate and the yellow copper chin straps.

1st Eclaireur regiment: Young Guard Squadrons

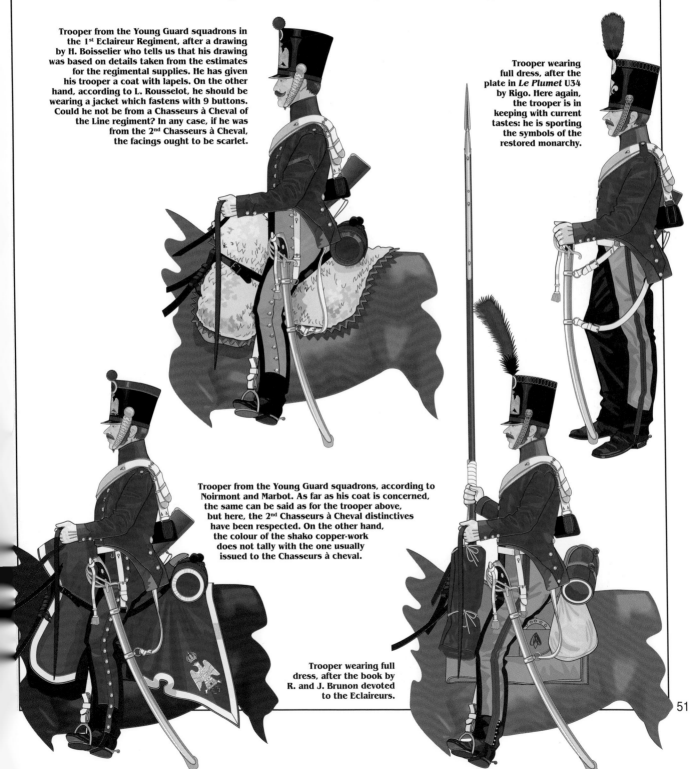

Trooper from the Young Guard squadrons in the 1st Eclaireur Regiment, after a drawing by H. Boisselier who tells us that his drawing was based on details taken from the estimates for the regimental supplies. He has given his trooper a coat with lapels. On the other hand, according to L. Rousselot, he should be wearing a jacket which fastens with 9 buttons. Could he not be from a Chasseurs à Cheval of the Line regiment? In any case, if he was from the 2nd Chasseurs à Cheval, the facings ought to be scarlet.

Trooper wearing full dress, after the plate in *Le Plumet* U34 by Rigo. Here again, the trooper is in keeping with current tastes: he is sporting the symbols of the restored monarchy.

Trooper from the Young Guard squadrons, according to Noirmont and Marbot. As far as his coat is concerned, the same can be said as for the trooper above, but here, the 2nd Chasseurs à Cheval distinctives have been respected. On the other hand, the colour of the shako copper-work does not tally with the one usually issued to the Chasseurs à cheval.

Trooper wearing full dress, after the book by R. and J. Brunon devoted to the Eclaireurs.

1st Eclaireur Regiment: Young Guard Squadrons

Adjudant Sous-Officier from the Eclaireurs of the Young Guard, after a drawing by H. Boisselier. He is wearing his three rank stripes in a V, above the coat facings. The white pompom on his shako indicates that he belongs to headquarters.

Trooper from the Eclaireurs of the Young Guard, after a drawing by F. Begnini. This trooper has probably come from a Chasseur à Cheval of the Line regiment, but strangely enough he is wearing a long coat with lapels, a model which was withdrawn in around 1810.

Trooper from the Eclaireurs of the Young Guard, after the engravings by Martinet.

The 1ˢᵗ Eclaireur Regiment: the Trumpeters

Trumpeter wearing full dress,
after a drawing by L. Rousselot.

Trumpeter wearing full dress,
after a drawing by H. Boisselier
taken from the estimates and
records of the regimental
supplies.

Brigadier-trompette in full dress, after the book
by R. and J. Brunon devoted to the Eclaireurs.
The tresses on the pelisse are white mixed with
sky blue. He is armed with a pistol hanging
from the shoulder strap by a snap hook.

53

The 1st Eclaireur Regiment: The Officers

Lieutenant wearing town dress, according to a drawing by H. Boisselier. This uniform is known to us thanks to a period miniature.

Uniform worn by Colonel Testot-Ferry, commanding the 1st Eclaireur Regiment, after a drawing by P. Begnini. His dress has all the items particular to senior officers. The only item of this splendid uniform to have survived is the dolman, now part of the Musée de l'Empéri Collection. Indeed Colonel Testot-Ferry did not wear it during the Campaign for France. For this he wore his pelisse. Unlike its owner, the aforementioned pelisse did not survive the 1814 campaign.

Lieutenant wearing campaign dress. The imagination officers used for their uniforms means that the fur borders on the pelisse were probably different colours.

Lieutenant in town dress. His uniform is identical to that above except for the shako which has been replaced by a hat and the sword by a sabre.

54

Clothing

Pelisse.

Dolman.

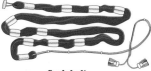

Sash-belt.

Hungarian breeches.

**Short-tailed coat
(*Habit-veste*) issued
to the two squadrons
of Young Guard.**

**Two types of riding breeches
used by the Eclaireurs
of the 1st Regiment.**

Shakos from the 1st Eclaireur Regiment.
Period documents show that different types
were worn: the 1812-model *(left)*
and the shako-rouleau *(right)*,
the same as the Hussars,
but shorter.

**Jacket
with sleeves.
Lucien
Rousselot
says that
the squadrons
of the Old Guard
probably wore a scarlet
jacket without sleeves.**

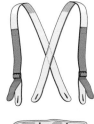

**Half-bell
buttons.**

Saddlery, Equipment and Weapons

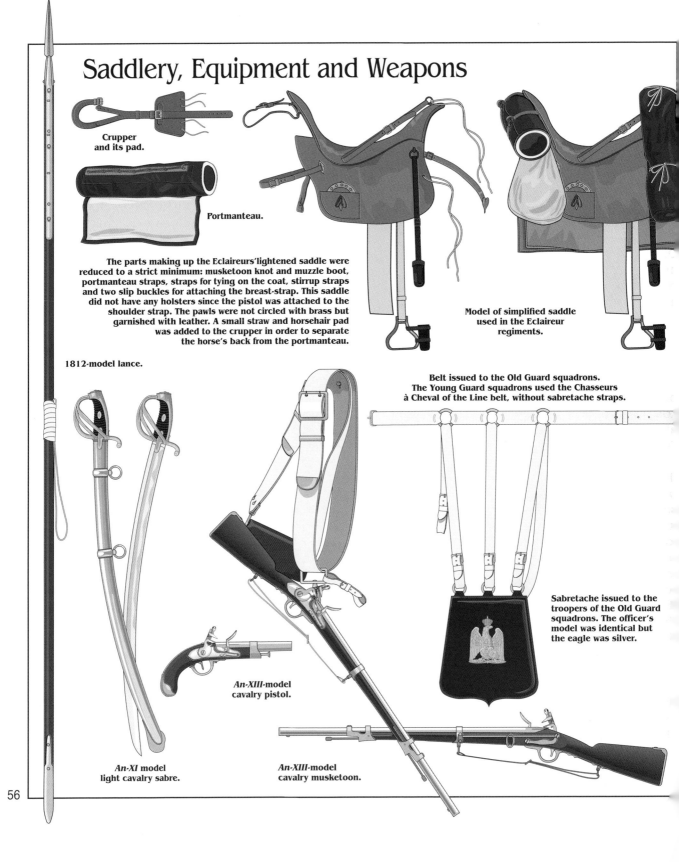

Crupper and its pad.

Portmanteau.

The parts making up the Eclaireurs' lightened saddle were reduced to a strict minimum: musketoon knot and muzzle boot, portmanteau straps, straps for tying on the coat, stirrup straps and two slip buckles for attaching the breast-strap. This saddle did not have any holsters since the pistol was attached to the shoulder strap. The pawls were not circled with brass but garnished with leather. A small straw and horsehair pad was added to the crupper in order to separate the horse's back from the portmanteau.

Model of simplified saddle used in the Eclaireur regiments.

1812-model lance.

Belt issued to the Old Guard squadrons. The Young Guard squadrons used the Chasseurs à Cheval of the Line belt, without sabretache straps.

Sabretache issued to the troopers of the Old Guard squadrons. The officer's model was identical but the eagle was silver.

***An-XIII*-model cavalry pistol.**

***An-XI* model light cavalry sabre.**

***An-XIII*-model cavalry musketoon.**

The 2ⁿᵈ Eclaireur Regiment

The 2ⁿᵈ Eclaireur Regiment was attached to the Dragoons of the Guard who provided some of the officers and men. The conscription and other units of the Line provided the rest: the 20ᵗʰ Dragoon Regiment, and the 3ʳᵈ and 7ᵗʰ Chevau-Léger sLancer Regiments. The 2ⁿᵈ Eclaireur Regiment was part of the Young Guard, except for the officers who came from the Old Guard.

The Eclaireurs-Dragons took part in the uninterrupted series of endless marches and battles during the Campaign for France until the end of March 1814. On 19 June 1814, at Poitiers, the regiment was dismissed by its Commanding Officer, Colonel-Major Hoffmayer. The remaining elements were transferred into the light cavalry of the Line.

The uniform of the 2ⁿᵈ Eclaireur Regiment

The Shako

According to contemporary documentation, two types of shako were worn. One was an inverted, sawn-off cone with the same peak as the infantry shakos. It was about the same size as the Hussars' shako-rouleau. The other was the classic shako-rouleau with a flat visor.

These shakos were covered with crimson cloth and their upper circumference was surrounded by a cloth band with a string of black rings, or according to certain sources, a plain aurora yellow stripe. The cockade was held in place by an aurora braid loop and a brass button. A pompom the colour of the squadron, and a white plume for full dress, surmounted the whole. The chinstrap comprised a small brass chain on a leather strip. An aurora cord was attached to the upper rear part of the shako and then worn saltire-wise, thus preventing the trooper from losing his hat. There was a black leather square at the rear of the hat to protect the nape.

The Coat

The coat with short tails (habit-veste) fastened down the front by means of 9 brass buttons. The collar, facings, turnbacks and piping were crimson. The shoulder flaps were green with crimson borders.

Trousers

These were cut from green cloth with a double crimson stripe down each side. Other types were used: trousers made of green cloth buttoning on the side with a crimson stripe, lined with black calfskin; or trousers just like those worn by the 1ˢᵗ Regiment.

Equipment

This was made of white or black, unstitched buffalo hide and comprised a cartridge-case and its shoulder strap, and a musketoon-holder strap.

The belt was the one used by the Chasseurs à Cheval of the Line.

Weapons

The ranks of Lancers were equipped with the 1812-model Lance and an An-XIII-model pistol hanging from the shoulder strap. The Carabinier ranks were armed with the An-XIII-model musketoon. They were all armed with an An-XI-model light cavalry sabre.

Saddlery

Like the 1ˢᵗ Regiment, two types of saddles were used: the classic-Hungarian-style-model with a striped green shabrack; and the lighter version with leather panels, placed on a blanket. Both were presumably used as there is quite a lot of uncertainty on this point.

The Trumpeters

They have something in common with most Trumpeters in the Guard: the colour of their uniform. The short-tailed coat was sky blue with a crimson distinctive, and a gold function stripe on the collar and facings. Strangely enough, the Trompette-Major is wearing a coat cut according to the 1812 regulations, but with crimson lapels, after a drawing by E. Lelièpvre which appeared in the magazine Le Passepoil.

The Officers

They wore the same uniform as the troopers but it was made of finer cloth with gold rank epaulettes. All the ornamentation on the shako was either gold trimming or gold metal. The trousers were made of green cloth with a crimson side stripe.

The buckles of the harness were gold. The shabrack was made of green cloth decorated with a single gold stripe and in the rear corners there was an eagle with gold trimmings.

The 2nd Eclaireur Regiment

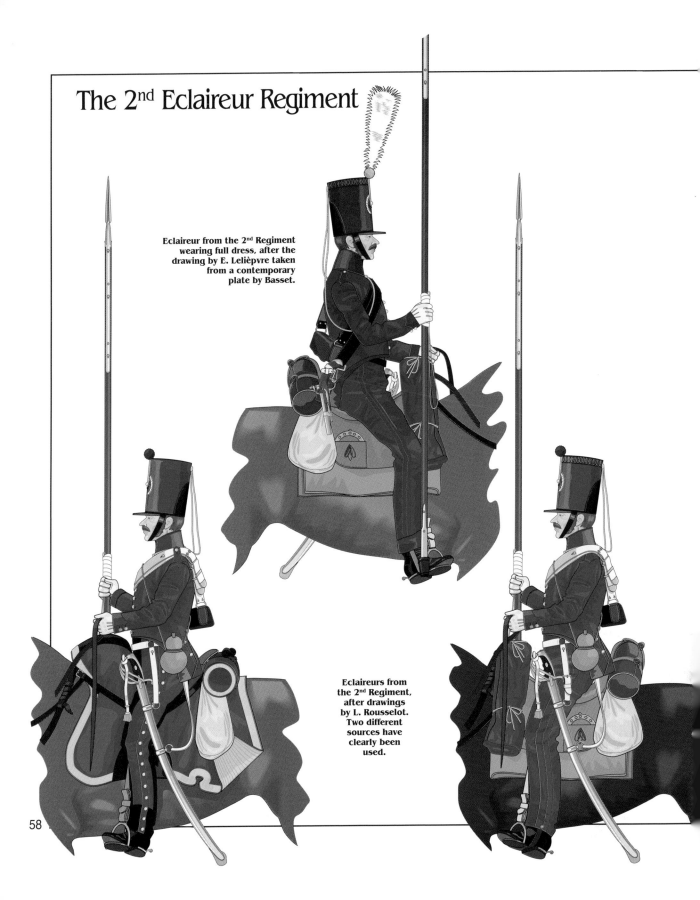

Eclaireur from the 2nd Regiment wearing full dress, after the drawing by E. Lelièpvre taken from a contemporary plate by Basset.

Eclaireurs from the 2nd Regiment, after drawings by L. Rousselot. Two different sources have clearly been used.

The 2ⁿᵈ Eclaireur Regiment

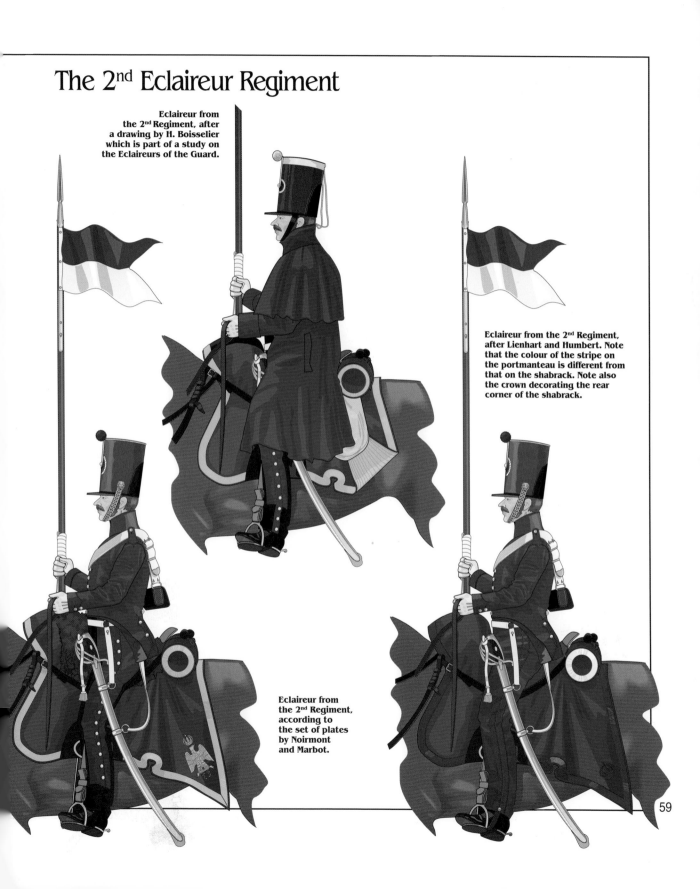

Eclaireur from the 2ⁿᵈ Regiment, after a drawing by H. Boisselier which is part of a study on the Eclaireurs of the Guard.

Eclaireur from the 2ⁿᵈ Regiment, after Lienhart and Humbert. Note that the colour of the stripe on the portmanteau is different from that on the shabrack. Note also the crown decorating the rear corner of the shabrack.

Eclaireur from the 2ⁿᵈ Regiment, according to the set of plates by Noirmont and Marbot.

The 2nd Eclaireur Regiment

Cylindrical shako-rouleau with flat visor, like the one worn by certain Hussar regiments at the end of the Empire.

Inverted cone-shaped shako. The smallest diameter of the hat is at the top. The St. Cyr cadets wear the same shape hats though they are smaller.

The two types of shako worn by the 2nd Regiment Eclaireurs. Note the aurora yellow cord attached to the rear of the hat: worn saltire-wise round the troopers chest, it prevented the trooper losing it.

Habit-veste of the 2nd Eclaireur Regiment.

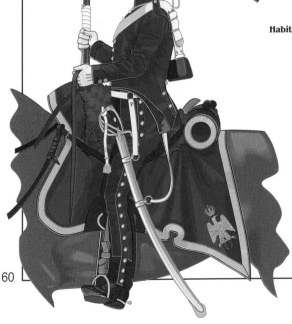

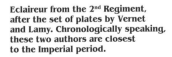

Eclaireur from the 2nd Regiment, according to a study by H. Boisselier who gives an original drawing in the Darmstadt Cabinet as his source.

Eclaireur from the 2nd Regiment, after the set of plates by Vernet and Lamy. Chronologically speaking, these two authors are closest to the Imperial period.

The 2ⁿᵈ Eclaireur Regiment: the Trumpeters

Trumpeter from the 2ⁿᵈ Regiment, according to a drawing by P. Begnini.

Trumpet-Major from the 2ⁿᵈ Regiment, according to a drawing by E. Lelièpvre which appeared in *Le Passepoil*. The gold stripes correspond to the rank of *Maréchal-des-Logis Chef*. They are above the facing which itself is decorated with a stripe indicating the Trumpeter's role. The white pompom indicates that he belonged to regimental headquarters.

***Brigadier-Trompette* from the 2ⁿᵈ Regiment, after a drawing by L. Rousselot. The position of the stripes on the sleeves is the same as for the Trumpet-Major, but here they are gold.**

Trumpeter from the 2ⁿᵈ Regiment, according to a drawing by E. Lelièpvre appearing in the magazine *Le Passepoil*.

The 2ⁿᵈ Eclaireur Regiment: the Officers

Junior officer from
the 2ⁿᵈ Regiment wearing
full dress, after the work
by R. and J. Brunon on
the Eclaireurs of the Guard.

Major (Second Colonel) of the
2ⁿᵈ Eclaireur Regiment according
to a drawing by H. Boisselier, after
the Valmont Collection. He is wearing a
coat with straight lapels. The epaulettes
denoting his rank consisted of a silver
embroidered body and fringes with large
gold cabled braid. All the trimmings
on his equipment were gold with green
stripes. The shabrack did not have the
double stripe normally used by senior
officers. Note the embroidery on the
shabrack as well as the eagle
adorning the portmanteau.

The 3rd Eclaireur Regiment

The 3rd Eclaireur Regiment was placed directly under Major-General Krasinski, commanding the 1st Polish Chevau-Légers Regiment of the Guard to which it was attached.

As a result no colonel was appointed and Squadron Commander Kozietulski was made Regimental Major. The officers and the NCOs came mostly from the Old Guard and notably from the 1st Polish Chevau-Légers. The troopers came from the same regiment's last companies which were considered Young Guard. Numbers were made up with men from the Polish corps depot at Sedan and then with French recruits from the Courbevoie depot.

As and when they were formed, the 3rd Regiment squadrons joined the army; the new recruits were instructed on the way. The 3rd Eclaireur Regiment was part of General Pac's division which comprised the 1st Chevau-Légers, the Krakus and the Lithuanian Tartars.

They fought on 11 February 1814 at Champaubert. When Napoleon abdicated, the regiment's French troopers were dismissed; the Poles were released from their oath and returned to Poland with elements of the 1st Chevau-Légers.

The uniform of the 3rd Eclaireur Regiment

The 3rd Regiment Eclaireurs' uniform was essentially the same as that of the 1st Chevau-Légers Regiment to which they were attached. But it cost a lot less. Besides there were a few details to distinguish it from the Old Guard's uniform.

The Czapka

This was the same shape as that of the Old Guard but it cost half the price. Moreover, the crowned **N** on the front plate was replaced by four crossed lances surmounted by an eagle. There was no plume, but a pompom the colour of the squadron.

The Kurtka

There wasn't much difference with the one worn by the Old Guard, save the quality of the cloth. The Polish Eclaireurs wore a pair of white woollen epaulettes. As for the conscripts, their shoulder flaps were blue with crimson borders. All of them wore a white cloth belt with three blue stripes that fastened over the kurtka and hid the sabre-holder belt.

Trousers

These were made of grey linen; there were no side stripes. There was a black calfskin lining between the legs.

Equipment and Weapons

These were the same as for the 2nd Eclaireur Regiment. Weapons were issued in the same way as for the 1st and 2nd Regiments.

Saddlery

The Eclaireurs of the 3rd Regiment used the same saddles as the 1st and 2nd Regiments: the classic Hungarian-style model and the lighter model with leather panels.

On the other hand, according to period pictures and supply reports, the different types of harnesses used seem to depend on which depot the Eclaireurs came from: sheepskin shabrack for the French conscripts from the Courbevoie depot, dark blue cloth shabrack for the Eclaireurs from the Polish troops' general depot at Sedan.

The Trumpeters

Their czapkas were white, but decorated differently depending on the source. Moreover, there were two types of kurtka: one was sky blue and the other white. The latter was worn with blue trousers like those worn by the 1st Regiment Chevau-Légers but with blue cord between two white stripes down the side. Different recruitment origins could explain this disparity, but there is no certainty about this.

The NCOs and Officers

These mostly came from the 1st Chevau-Légers Regiment. They kept their uniforms, equipment and weapons without changing anything.

According to the iconography, only officers wearing campaign dress have been attested. Moreover, it is not known whether junior officers originating from other units wore Polish-style uniforms.

The 3rd Eclaireur Regiment

Maréchal-des-Logis in the 3rd Eclaireurs. Like all the officers coming from the ranks of the 1st Polish Chevau-Légers, he has kept his uniform without changing anything.

Eclaireur from the 3rd Regiment, after a drawing by L. Rousselot.

Two Eclaireurs from the 3rd Regiment, according to a drawing by H. Boisselier who made it after a document in the Marbot Collection. These troopers apparently come from the Polish troop depot at Sedan.

The 3rd Eclaireur Regiment

Eclaireur from the 3rd Regiment wearing stable dress, taken from the Millot Collection, after a drawing by Rupniewski. He was probably originally from the 1st Chevau-Légers Regiment since he is wearing their uniform.

Eclaireur from the 3rd Regiment, according to a study by H. Boisselier based on the supply reports. This is a French conscript from the Courbevoie depot.

Eclaireur from the 3rd Regiment, after a drawing by P. Begnini.

Eclaireur from the 3rd Regiment, according to a study by H. Boisselier based on the supply reports. This is a French conscript from the Courbevoie depot.

The 3ʳᵈ Eclaireur Regiment: the Trumpeters

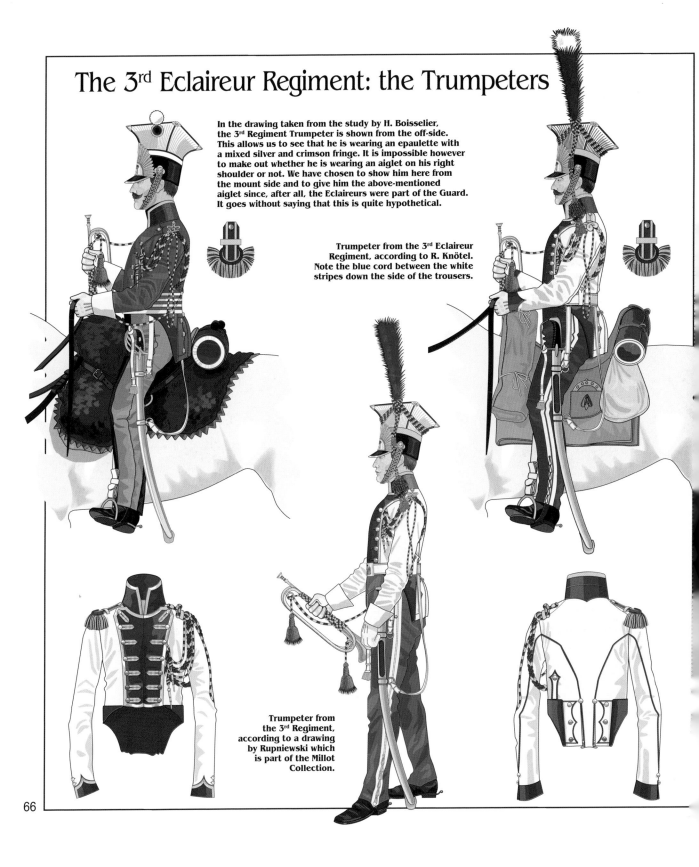

In the drawing taken from the study by H. Boisselier, the 3ʳᵈ Regiment Trumpeter is shown from the off-side. This allows us to see that he is wearing an epaulette with a mixed silver and crimson fringe. It is impossible however to make out whether he is wearing an aiglet on his right shoulder or not. We have chosen to show him here from the mount side and to give him the above-mentioned aiglet since, after all, the Eclaireurs were part of the Guard. It goes without saying that this is quite hypothetical.

Trumpeter from the 3ʳᵈ Eclaireur Regiment, according to R. Knötel. Note the blue cord between the white stripes down the side of the trousers.

Trumpeter from the 3ʳᵈ Regiment, according to a drawing by Rupniewski which is part of the Millot Collection.

The 3rd Eclaireur Regiment: the Officers

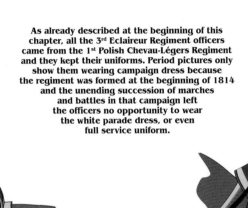

As already described at the beginning of this chapter, all the 3rd Eclaireur Regiment officers came from the 1st Polish Chevau-Légers Regiment and they kept their uniforms. Period pictures only show them wearing campaign dress because the regiment was formed at the beginning of 1814 and the unending succession of marches and battles in that campaign left the officers no opportunity to wear the white parade dress, or even full service uniform.

Officer from the 3rd Eclaireur Regiment wearing campaign dress, after a drawing by P. Begnini.

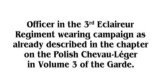

Officer in the 3rd Eclaireur Regiment wearing campaign as already described in the chapter on the Polish Chevau-Léger in Volume 3 of the Garde.

Clothing, Equipment and Weapons

Czapka
belonging to
the 3rd Regiment.

Decorative
front plate.

The cartridge case,
its shoulder strap and
the musketoon-holder
belt which the Lancers
also used to hang
their only pistol
from.

NCO's kurtka.
Officers kept their
Old Guard uniform.

An-XIII-model
cavalry pistol.

Kurtka belonging
to an Eclaireur of
Polish origin.

Note the difference in cut of
the lapels on these two kurtkas.
The blue-striped white belt was
common to all the Eclaireurs
no matter where or how
they were recruited.

Kurtka belonging to
a conscript Eclaireur
of French origin.

Riding
breeches.

Sabre-holder belt.

An-XI-model
cavalry
sabre.

1812-model lance
with its taffeta
pennant.

An-XIII-model
cavalry musketoon.

68

The HORSE ARTILLERY

Originating with the Consular Guard, the Horse Artillery of the Imperial Guard started as a company, became a squadron in 1802, then a regiment after the 15 April 1806 reorganisation. The regiment consisted of three squadrons of two 97-men companies, plus 25 Velites. With the creation of the Artillery Regiment in 1808, the Horse Artillery was reduced to two 2-company squadrons. When the Guard was reorganised in 1813, the regiment grew to three 2-squadron companies with the number of guns rising from 120 to 190, shared out among 26 batteries. A Young Guard Horse Artillery company was created at the end of 1813. The regiment was laid off in July 1814 only to be re-formed in 1815, this time with four companies of four 6-gun batteries.

The Horse Artillery Uniform

The Colback

In shape and size this was the same as that of the Chasseurs à Cheval. All the adornments were scarlet, traditionally the artillery's distinctive colour. A pendant, a cord, two flounders with tassels and a tricolour cockade with a yellow woollen 'N' in the centre adorned the colback. The chin straps were made of leather covered with a little brass chain. When campaign dress was worn all the decorations were removed and the pendant was replaced by a leather cap fastened to the top of the crown used as backing.

The Dolman and the Pelisse

Cut just like those of the Chasseurs à Cheval but dark blue in colour, they had 18 rows of braid and three of round buttons; they were used until the end of the Empire. The *Brigadier*'s stripes were sewn above the facings. At the beginning of the Empire the sash-belt, worn over the dolman, was dark blue with scarlet loops; it was subsequently scarlet with bright yellow loops.

The waistcoat

This was sleeveless and collarless, and garnished with scarlet braid and three rows of buttons. Under the service or campaign dress waistcoat, the gunner wore a sleeveless jacket fastened with two rows of buttons but without braid. Stable dress included a dark blue double-breasted jacket with sleeves, fastening with two rows of buttons.

The Coat

When wearing campaign dress, the gunner changed his far too fragile Hussar-style uniform for a dark-blue *"à la Chasseur"* coat with scarlet distinctives. With this uniform he wore an aiglet—to show he belonged to the Guard—on his left shoulder.

The Breeches

These were cut *"à la Hongroise"*; they were dark blue with scarlet trimmings. For the campaign dress, dark blue riding breeches were worn. They had scarlet stripes down the side and fastened with brass buttons. They were lined with blackened calfskin.

The Equipment

This was identical to that of the Chasseurs à Cheval *(see Volume 2 of the Garde)*, except for the musketoon-holder strap which, as the musketoon was not issued to this arm, was of no use. At the beginning of the Empire the sabretache was covered in dark blue cloth with scarlet stripes and decorated with an embroidered emblem. Because this was too fragile, it was replaced by an insignia cut out of brass showing an eagle surmounting two crossed cannon.

Weapons

At the beginning of the Empire, the weapon issued was probably an *An-XI*-model Hussar sabre. Subsequently the Horse Gunners were given the same sabre as the Chasseurs à Cheval of the Guard. They were also armed with a pair of *An-XIII*-model pistols.

The NCOs

They wore the same uniform as the troopers. The dolmans and the pelisses were decorated with mixed scarlet and gold. Their stripes were worn above the facings of the dolman and the coat, and repeated on the pelisse above the facing stripe. All the NCOs wore the same uniform.

FULL DRESS

Horse Artillery of the Guard sabretaches.
On the left, the first model with embroidered
emblems. On the right, the second model
with cut-out copper emblem.

Gunner from the Horse
Artillery of the Guard wearing
full parade dress, after plate
N° 60 in *"L'Armée Française"*
by Lucien Rousselot, and
a plate by Michel Pétard
appearing in N° 91
of *"Uniformes"*
magazine.

The Horse Artillery of the Guard
mounted dark bay
or black horses.

CAMPAIGN AND SERVICE DRESS

Gunner wearing
service dress.

Gunner, First Class,
after L. Rousselot.

Gunner during
the 1806-1807
campaigns,
according to
L. Rousselot.

Gunner wearing
a cloak-coat.

CAMPAIGN AND SERVICE DRESS

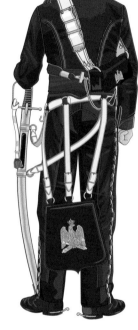

Brigadier wearing
campaign dress,
towards the end
of the Empire.

Sabretache carried towards
the end of the Empire. This model
was made of leather; it was less
fragile than the previous model
and bore the same emblem
cut-out of copper.

Purveyor-server-gunner wearing exercise
dress. He is wearing the sleeveless plain
blue jacket fastening down the front with
brass buttons, and leather-lined riding
trousers. He is carrying a bag over his
shoulder holding cannon ball cartridges
which he supplies to the first left-hand
server while the gun is being served.

Gunner in the Horse Artillery
of the Young Guard, towards 1814.
His very much simplified uniform
consists of a coat buttoning straight
down and riding breeches. He is armed
with an *An-XIII*-model light cavalry
sabre. The cartridge case and its
shoulder strap are the models used
by the light cavalry.

The SECOND UNIFORM AND SOCIAL DRESS

Gunner from the Horse
Artillery wearing social
dress, according to plate
N° 60 by L. Rousselot.

Gunner from the Horse
Artillery, after the Weiland
Manuscript, towards 1807.
Note the rounded edge at
the top of the lapels, the
pompom on the colback and
the plume, placed on the
front of the headdress, and
the sabre-knot, all
entirely scarlet.

Horse Artillery gunner wearing his pelisse.
Under the pelisse, he is wearing only a waistcoat.
Because the pelisse was so tightly-fitting, it was
impossible to wear the dolman and sash under it.
The Horse Artillery also used a black plume
with scarlet tip.

Horse Gunner,
according to Henschel,
about 1807.

Horse Gunner wearing
social dress in summer.
He is wearing breeches
and a waistcoat cut
from cotton cloth
which was lighter than
the ordinary cloth.

ITEMS OF CLOTHING

Dolman with eighteen rows of braid and three of buttons.

Cockade.

Horse Artillery of the Guard colback.
It comprised a bearskin mounted on a strong leather body. The hair was combed downwards. The inside was garnished with soft leather and canvas. The top was filled by the pendant which fastened onto the body. With the campaign dress, the pendant was replaced by a leather cap which was fastened to the same spot.

 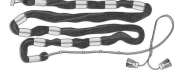

Horse Artillery of the Guard sash-belt. On the left the model used at the beginning of the Empire.

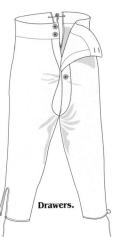

Shirt.

Uniform buttons

Pelisse with eighteen rows of braid and three of buttons. The model remained unchanged throughout the Empire.

Drawers.

"A la dragonne" forage cap.

Waistcoat with scarlet braid, worn under the coat with the second uniform.

Waistcoat worn as part of quarters or manœuvres dress.

Hungarian breeches.

Riding breeches.

74

ITEMS OF CLOTHING

Young Guard Gunners' shako. We have tried to reconstitute it from a description by L. Rousselot.

Hat worn with social dress.

Gunner's aiglet.

Uniform buttons.

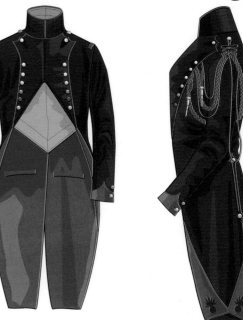

Coat-Overcoat attributed to the Gunners of the Young Guard in the 1813 formations. It has two piped scarlet shoulder flaps. Under this overcoat, the Gunner wore the plain blue sleeveless waistcoat with two rows of buttons.

"A la Chasseur" second uniform. There were two types of collar, closed and pinned like the one above, or open. Note that the real pockets were on the inside of the turnback.

1   2   3   4   5   6

Ranks markings:

1. Gunner with one seniority stripe for 10 years' service.
2. Gunner, First Class (the two stripes were only worn on the left sleeve) with two chevrons for 10 to 20 years' service.
3. *Brigadier* (the two stripes were worn on both sleeves) with more than 20 to 25 years' service.
4. *Maréchal-des-Logis* with seniority stripes.
5. *Maréchal-des-Logis Chef.*
6. *Adjudant.*

EQUIPMENT AND WEAPONS

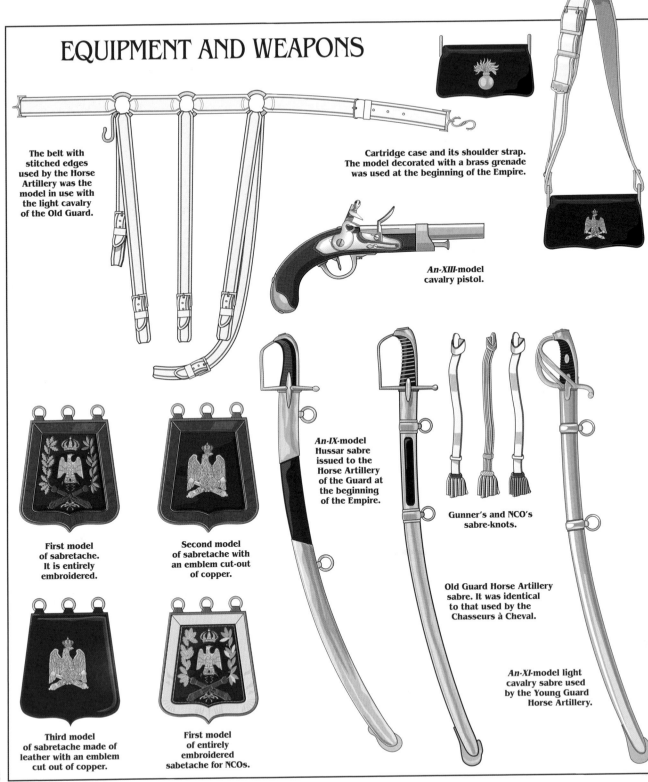

The belt with stitched edges used by the Horse Artillery was the model in use with the light cavalry of the Old Guard.

Cartridge case and its shoulder strap. The model decorated with a brass grenade was used at the beginning of the Empire.

An-XIII-model cavalry pistol.

An-IX-model Hussar sabre issued to the Horse Artillery of the Guard at the beginning of the Empire.

Gunner's and NCO's sabre-knots.

First model of sabretache. It is entirely embroidered.

Second model of sabretache with an emblem cut-out of copper.

Old Guard Horse Artillery sabre. It was identical to that used by the Chasseurs à Cheval.

Third model of sabretache made of leather with an emblem cut out of copper.

First model of entirely embroidered sabetache for NCOs.

An-XI-model light cavalry sabre used by the Young Guard Horse Artillery.

HARNESSES

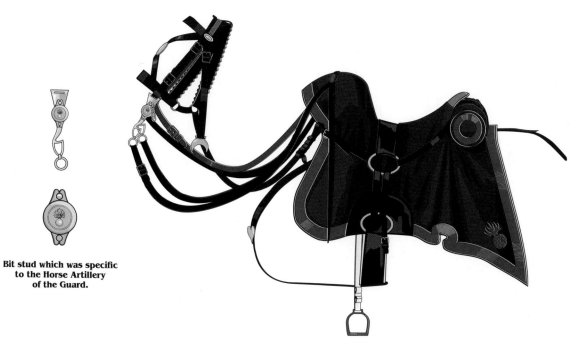

**Bit stud which was specific
to the Horse Artillery
of the Guard.**

Hungarian-style saddle and harness of the Horse Artillery of the Guard.
This saddlery has already been described earlier *(in Volumes 1 and 2 on the Cavalry
of the Guard)*. The only differences were the bits which were specific to the Horse Artillery.
Other models have been encountered. The dark blue shabrack has scarlet striping and
is decorated with a red grenade in the rear corners. This harness remained unchanged
during the whole of the Empire. Note the scarlet parade halter.

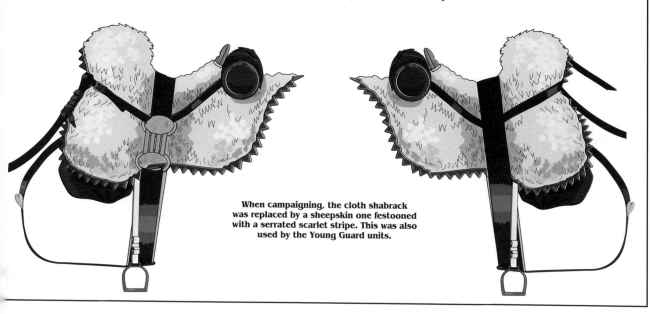

When campaigning, the cloth shabrack
was replaced by a sheepskin one festooned
with a serrated scarlet stripe. This was also
used by the Young Guard units.

GRIBEAUVAL'S SYSTEM 8-POUNDER

In the French appellation "pièce de 8" (8-pounder), the figure 8 refers to the weight of the cannonball in pounds, not the calibre. The 8-pounder cannonball weighed 3.912 kg (1 lb = 0.489 g).
We will have the opportunity to return to the different parts that went to making up Gribeauval's system in the next volume which will continue our study of the Horse Artillery of the Guard.

Eight-pounder mounted on its front axle.
In this the road position, the canon rested on the rear recesses of the carriage. It was repositioned into the front recesses when ready for firing.

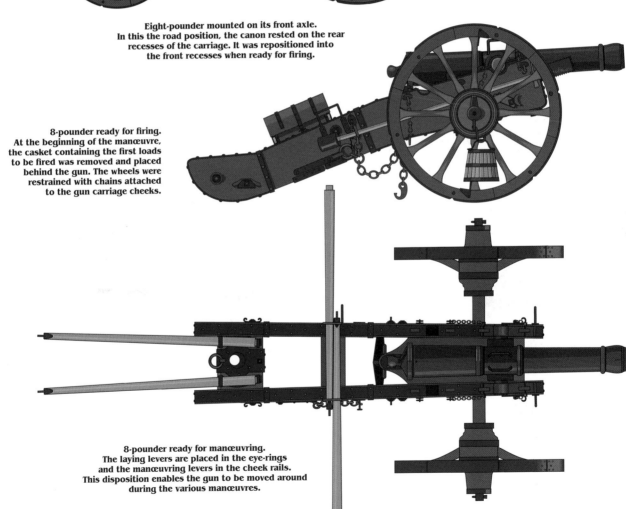

8-pounder ready for firing.
At the beginning of the manœuvre, the casket containing the first loads to be fired was removed and placed behind the gun. The wheels were restrained with chains attached to the gun carriage cheeks.

8-pounder ready for manœuvring.
The laying levers are placed in the eye-rings and the manœuvring levers in the cheek rails.
This disposition enables the gun to be moved around during the various manœuvres.

NCOs IN FULL DRESS

NCO wearing full parade dress after L. Rousselot. All the trimmings are a mix of scarlet and gold. Note the two variants in the position of the *Maréchal-des-Logis'* stripes. In theory all NCOs wore the same uniform.

NCOs WEARING CAMPAIGN DRESS

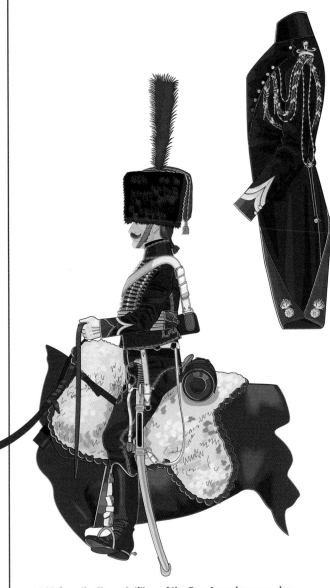

"A la Chasseur" coat belonging to a *Maréchal-des-Logis*. Unlike normal practice in the other corps of the Guard, the Horse Artillery NCOs wore the same aiglet no matter what their rank was.

Maréchal-des-Logis Chef wearing a frock-coat, after L. Rousselot.

NCO from the Horse Artillery of the Guard wearing campaign dress during the 1806 campaign. We have tried to reconstitute this uniform after a painting by P.A. Vafflard called the *"Colonne de Rossbach"* in the Versailles Museum. In it, the Horse Artillery of the Guard appears in the background, accompanied by the artillery train. This NCO is wearing a dolman and Hungarian breeches. A certain number of artillerymen did not in fact wear their sabretaches. On the other hand all of them wore the scarlet plume and the colback pendant.

Maréchal-des-Logis wearing campaign dress, after L. Rousselot.

TRUMPETER IN FULL PARADE DRESS

Trumpeter from the Horse Artillery
of the Guard wearing full parade
dress, in about 1807,
after plate N° 74
in *"L'Armée Française"*
by Lucien Rousselot.

BIBLIOGRAPHY

Planches « Uniformes de l'Armée française » par Lucien Rousselot
— La Gendarmerie d'élite. Planche n° 95.
— L'artillerie à cheval de la Garde, planches n° 60 et n° 74.

Planches « Le Plumet » par Rigo
— Gendarmerie d'élite de la Garde, timbalier en 1806, Planche n° 6.
— Gendarmes d'ordonnance, trompette, 1809, Planche n° 176
— 1er Régiment d'éclaireurs, officiers et cavaliers, 1814, Planche n° U 34.
— Tartares lithuaniens, cavaliers en 1813-1814, Planche n° 105.
— Tartares lithuaniens, chef d'escadron en grande tenue, 1813, Planche n° 228.

**Fiches documentaires « Les soldats du temps jadis »
par Roger Forthoffer, chez l'auteur.**
— Les tartares lithuaniens, fiches n° 264 et n° 265.

Livres
— Soldats et uniformes du Premier Empire, les krakus polonais,
Dr F.-G. Hourtoulle, J. Girbal ; P. Courcelle. *Histoire & Collections.*
— Les gardes d'honneurs pendant la campagne de 1813-1814.
Editions Librairie Teissèdre.
— La Garde Impériale,
L. Fallou. *Editions J. Olmes* (réédition).
— La Garde impériale,
Noirmont et Marbot. *Bibliothèque du musée de l'Armée.*
— La Garde impériale,
Marco de Saint-Hilaire. *Musée de l'Armée.*
— Armorial du Ier Empire,
de Vaulchier, J.-J. Lartigue, P. Binet. *Editions Alsyd.*
— Armes à feu réglementaires françaises 1717-1836, J. Boudriot.
— Equipement militaire. 1600-1870.Tome IV,
M. Pétard. *Chez l'auteur.*

— Des sabres et des épées,
M. Pétard. *Editions du Canonnier.*
— Drapeaux et étendards du Premier Empire,
P. Charrié. *Editions Copernic.*
— Garde Impériale, Les éclaireurs,
Collection Raoul et Jean Brunon, Marseille.
— Napoléon et ses soldats,
Collection historique du Musée de l'Armée. *Editions Préal.*
— Manuscrit du camp de Dresde,
Sauerweid. *Editions Pierre Brétegnier.*
— Le manuscrit de Markolsheim,
transcription de R. Forthoffer. *Chez l'auteur, 1961.*
— Manuscrit du canonnier Hahlo,
R. Forthoffer. *Chez l'auteur, 1973.*
— Les uniformes et armes des soldats du Premier Empire,
L. & F. Funcken. *Editions Castermann.*
— Napoleon's army,
A. Martinet & G, Dempsey. *Editions Greenhill Books.*
— Napoleonic uniforms,
J. Elting & R. Knötel. *Editions MacMillan.*
— Napoléon's guard of honour,
R. Pawley, P. Courcelle. *Osprey n° 378.*

Revues
— Le gendarme d'élite, M. Pétard in *Uniformes* n° 90.
— L'artilleur à cheval de la Garde, M. Pétard in *Uniformes* n° 74.
— Les Gardes d'honneur, Christian Blondiau in *Uniformes* n° 47.
— Les Gardes d'honneurs, J.-P. Tarin, in *bulletin du CFFH.*
— Le 1er régiment d'éclaireurs, Lucien Rousselot in *Uniformes* n° 9
— *Bulletins du CFFH,* années 1971-1972.

ACKNOWLEDGEMENTS

We would like to thank Rigo, Michel Pétard, Dr François-Guy Hourtoulle, M. Lapray, Denis Gandilhon and Jean-Louis Viau for their precious help as much morale-wise as editorially. We would like to pay them the tribute which they deserve.

Design, creation, lay-out and realisation by ANDRE JOUINEAU and JEAN-MARIE MONGIN.
Re-reading and updating by Jean-Louis VIAU. © *Histoire & Collections* 2006
Computer Drawings by André JOUINEAU

ISBN : 2-35250-002-8

Publish number: 2-35250

Un ouvrage édité par
HISTOIRE & COLLECTIONS
SA au capital de 182938, 82 €
5, avenue de la République F-75541 Paris Cédex 11

▶ **N° Indigo** 0 820 888 911
0,118 € TTC / MN

Fax 0147005111
www.histoireetcollections.fr

This book has been designe
typed, laid-out and processe
by *Histoire & Collection*
fully on integrate
computer equipme

Printed by QUEBECC
Spain, European Uni
September 200